Just a girl from Crewe

Janice Madden

First published   September 2005
By   Kitestring Publishing,
                 GPO Box 536   ADELAIDE
                 South Australia   5001
                 kitestringpublisher@yahoo.com.au

The stories: -

- The Guinea Pig Girl
- The Paper Cranes
- Our Neighbour
- The Dinner Lady
- Our Venture
- Two Poets

have previously been published in 2004 as an anthology of short stories entitled Circles Within Circles.

Inquiries should be addressed to the publisher

Printed by Eagle Press, Adelaide, South Australia
Typeset layout by Ailsa Williams

ISBN 0-9757903-0-7

Just a Girl From Crewe

Homeland from Afar

Homeland From Afar

The jet flew on through the night, while cocooned in their blankets the passengers slept, oblivious to the great moon, which lit up the skies and massive mountain ranges below.

From my window seat I peered down at the incredible landscape, noting the silver rivers defining the valleys dwarfed by inhospitable crags towering on every side. Occasionally we flew over isolated villages, revealed by pinpoints of light, which were quickly blotted out by low cloud.

What was happening down there in those small isolated villages, I wondered? How did the women and children manage to live surrounded by the effects of war?

Hearing excited whispers from the crew who were peering through the windows, I joined them. They explained that they had never flown over Afghanistan before. The airline had only recently been given airspace as the Russians had withdrawn from this inaccessible country. At that moment I made a vow that night to learn more about Afghanistan.

In 2001 I was given the opportunity when I worked with Afghan women in South Australia. As we talked together I remembered the flight over their inhospitable country and the urge to know more about their homeland was reunited in me.

Most of the women came from Kabul. Many were illiterate in their own written language and all of them were anxious to learn English. We talked about their wild country dominated by tribal wars and their concerns for their remaining family in their homeland.

They described small farms where they struggled to survive on insufficient food. One woman, anxious to explain her story, sketched a crude drawing of a large wood-burning stove onto the white board in the classroom. We all listened in amazement to her faltering words as some of the women helped her out with a handful of recently acquired words of English.

"No fire in the day-time. Soldiers banged on the door looking for my son to join their fighters. He was twelve years old my son. I pushed him into the large oven. My husband stood in front of it."

"'Where is your son Khalid? We know he is here.' My husband raised his eyes to the ceiling and shook his head. They knocked him about with the gun."

"Where? Where is he?" they shouted. "Tell us or we will shoot you."

She covered her face with her trembling hands, remembering everything. "They shot him in front of me," she cried. "They shot my husband and left our home."

Her son, crouched on the still warm ashes, heard the gunshot.

She continued. "Late that night when I had covered my husband's body, we left – just the two of us, over the mountains. We began our long journey. We did not dare stay - even to bury him."

So the stories came tumbling out. I began to form pictures of their villages, their families, the food they ate and their traditional way of life disintegrating around them.

One day I confided in the woman that I was suffering from toothache. To my amazement everyone began to laugh. Immediately they gave me graphic and colourful accounts of their village dentist who doubled up as the blacksmith. He was kept busy shoeing the horses across the street but he was called away several times each day to attend to rotting teeth and crying children.

rritated by the interruption, he forced open mouths with grubby hands unwashed from his previous work. Pulling of teeth from young and old commenced amidst screams and cries. Children were slapped for protesting and finally, blood-stained and cross, the 'dentist' wiped his hands on his bloodied apron before returning to his manlier job across the street!

My visit to the dentist that evening paled into insignificance!

Within the group was an older man from Kabul who had been a glassmaker from when he was a small boy. He described taking his hammer to smash his beautifully crafted glasswork before he fled from his shop. Together we cried as he re-enacted the destruction of his and his ancestors' work in a moment of despair.

When the media informed the world that the Buddhist statues of Kabul had been blown up from the rock faces by the Taliban, there was much discussion within the group. Many of the women had visited the statues, which had existed for thousands of years, and I expressed my regret over their destruction.

I was firmly put in my place.

"What about the people?" the Afghani women cried. "Why does no one know what is happening to our people? People are the ones who feel the suffering."

I came to love the beautiful dark eyed women who struggled to learn the concepts of a written and spoken language which was not their own. They still suffered with terrible headaches, the effects of malnutrition and previous tuberculosis. There were many lingering medical problems resulting from homebirths carried out by untrained midwives within the confines of their dark stone homes, on earth floors and without medication.

They were quick to point out to me that they were the lucky ones who had survived. Many women died giving birth.

I recall walking out into the sunshine of a bright Australian day, pointing up at the sky and saying "blue, blue sky," only to be met by a sad stare as an Afghani woman replied. "No, Janice. No God, no Allah."

Her suffering had been too great, finally leaving her numb with disbelief in any God.

Our happiest times spent together were during visits to their homes. Here, surrounded by their children, my friends relaxed. We talked about their childhoods and they urged me to tell them about mine.

I took photographs as a means of explanation. In return the women produced their worn-out but much treasured photos, which they had managed to carry with them from the old country to the new one.

We realized we had much in common for as I discovered them, they helped to unravel the past for me. And I realised that I didn't need to keep wandering. That there would always be somewhere over the horizon speaking to me and inviting me onward, but that I could now learn about it from all the people in my life that a girl from Crewe might never have been expected to meet.

Chapter One:

Beginning in 1940

Home to Crewe

You are holding tight a train ticket
re reading the destination
and finally believing it's coming true,
returning home, reconciling differences,
watching the wind sweep amber leaves
off the trees and not fearing winter.

Memories are excursions to childhood
village stations with rusting milk churns,
flowers in fire buckets
porters with nothing to do
and Father drives the engine
breathing her breath,
and you holding on to your suitcase
dreaming about the sea.

Today you are returning down
mind-tunnels and smoke screens
the past greeting the present.
apprehension mixed with expectation.

Leaning from the window
Crewe is as small as Wrens nest
a tangle of criss-cross lines
clearer and clearer
emotions change like signals
Arriving brings the
opening and slamming of doors
embraces and grasping of hands

Contentment is ambling home
arms linked without talking
happy in each others company
the crowds overtaking
and there is no need to hurry

Ryan Ó Conaill

My Father, George William Madden (1907 – 1977)

He died, sitting in an armchair in his front room, listening to the dawn chorus of birds. The disease that he had dreaded all his life, since it killed his mother, finally visited my beloved father to challenge his bravery and philosophy of living.

If there is such a thing as victory over death, then my father achieved it. His cancerous companion was acknowledged and experienced for many weeks until deterioration of his body necessitated an explanation to his family. He arranged his own funeral, even visiting the undertaker two weeks before his death.

When he sent for me to say goodbye, the day before he died, he was so in control of the human situation that I envied him. Serene, sensitive as always and somehow ageless, he held my hand and said farewell. He told me to get on with my life as he had done and I knew as I knelt down at the side of his chair, to be near to him, that he was far ahead of me, journeying on into eternity.

I remember feeling so weak, useless, totally a child before my father. I felt envy for his dignity and I wanted to walk by his side and go with him. Since he has died, this feeling has never left me. He is certainly at my side as I scurry and hurry about life's often trivial business.

Before I left him on that Sunday afternoon to catch the train back to Holyhead in North Wales, he asked to check my train ticket, something he had done automatically since my teenage years when I had travelled on a concession ticket allowed to family members of workers on the railway. It was such an ordinary little gesture, a sign that he was still looking after me even though I was a woman with three children.

The other thing that he asked me to do was to take a bunch of roses from his garden. Once again this had been a ritual in the summer and autumn months when I no longer lived at home. The normality of those two little actions in the face of death was beyond my comprehension.

I will always remember the lonely ride back to North Wales, clutching the roses and weeping in desperation, knowing that the journey was taking me further and further away from the person that I loved more than anyone or anything else on earth.

I remember looking out at the Cheshire fields wrapped in the evening mists of autumn. We passed Beeston, Bickerton, Peckforton, all the places where my father had roamed. I remember crying onto the roses, amongst them, Peace, which I had given to my father in 1963.

"Why? Why?" I screamed inwardly. That evening on the train I was so angry. Everything seemed meaningless. I needed my father. Why did he have to go now?

My earliest memories of my father are swathed in emotions stirred by the senses. He had a wonderful smell of rough tweed and of a healthy strong male body. His presence in the house was always felt, even when he was at work, which was frequent and continual.

My father was a handsome man. His high cheekbones, sharp blue eyes and lovely smile, which revealed incredibly strong white teeth, made me feel extremely proud of him.

I can remember a big hand holding mine as we trudged along Edleston Road in Crewe to the cinema on a winter's evening. I would drag behind, and my father would be a big warm presence at my side, willing me on. He was the light shining on the dark stairs. He frightened away my nightmares and fear of the dark. The bogeyman quailed before him.

My father required very little sleep, maybe only four or five hours a night, so he lived twice as long as everyone else. The dawn belonged to him. His sharp blue eyes would see the skein of geese winging their way across the sky in the early morning. His ears would hear that first birdcall, orchestrated into a symphony by nature. He would observe the delicate cobwebs trapping the night dew. His feet would walk on the earth, of which he is so much a part.

My father was at one with nature. He felt and understood the changing seasons, finding beauty and satisfaction in the icy winter days that temporarily laid to sleep all things growing. I can never recall him despising or grumbling at the inevitable toll of life. He understood the complexity of existence, and never challenging the inevitable. Rather, he was part of it, moving from winter to spring as naturally as a bud would open.

His love and joy of life revealed itself in many ways. His garden blossomed, his allotment swelled with vegetables, his pen captured all the senses. His shrewd wit revealed a deep understanding of the mysteries of human nature. Men loved and respected him but others feared him, as he could not be manipulated.

My father was a great worker and tremendous saver. Within four years of marrying my mother, he had paid for our family home. And what a home! It was filled with love. We were very much a family of four; my father, mother, sister and I, with an extended family of Grandmother and Aunty Cissy. It never really went beyond that for reasons which I did not discover until I was much older.

My father was an engine driver but once he arrived home, overalls were put into the shed and he became the poet, the storyteller and the provider of such security that sadness or worries never penetrated our world. Insecurity was something that did not exist.

The New Year was brought in by all the engine drivers who blew their whistles on hundreds of steam trains on the stroke of midnight. For miles around I could hear this eerie and exciting sound. Imagine how I felt when my father blew the whistle of his steam train, just for me, ten minutes before anyone else. For years I would lie in bed on New Year's Eve and wait for that special signal. When the sound pierced the silence of the night, I would laugh with delight.

Although I never really knew about his work, he gave me cameo pictures in the strangest of ways. On winter mornings I would come downstairs to a fire so large that it turned the living room into an oven! My father had "banked it up". I realised years later that it was a copycat of a steam engine fire!

One morning I came down to find several dead owls propped on the picture rails around the room. They stared at me with their large eyes, the bodies so downy and soft and no mark of death upon them. They had simply hit the train or lain in the track.

On other occasions I would find dead foxes or badgers, stretched out on the lawn. Quite often a small cardboard box in the kitchen would move slightly and I would rush forward to retrieve a hedgehog or grass snake.

Bunches of wild flowers would fill the house at springtime, alongside catkins and sticky buds. Deserted birds' nests would appear in the garden hedges and skinned rabbits would hang in the pantry, alongside an occasional pheasant and a side of bacon.

Long before the depletion of the ozone layer and the warnings of the environmentalists, my father handed me the book 'Silent Spring' by Rachel Carson. He said very little but grew deeply saddened as hedgehogs, frogs, newts, birds and wild flowers began to literally disappear from the Cheshire lanes in the 1960s.

I fell asleep every night listening to my father's voice telling me the most wonderful stories. Some of these were completed in a night but others carried on and I waited anxiously to hear the next episode. How clever my father was. All the tales had deeper meanings, giving me knowledge of life. As I matured, so did the stories, finally touching on the greatest mystery of life, love. Certainly the stories were not confined to England or to the present day. Always, they involved nature and certainly magic. The following day, unknowingly and subconsciously, I was affected by their tellings. Maybe I would be a little kinder to my playmates, not resist change and discipline or look beyond the obvious explanation. Father gave me wisdom in this way.

I would resist sleep for a long time by squeezing my eyes shut and pinching my arms. I could hear my father's beautiful soft voice and I would think that I was imagining him as I absorbed the words. I would poke down in the bed under the heavy blankets and finally come to a stop when I felt the body of my father lying far down across the bottom of the bed. How cold he must have felt on winter nights, as I lay tucked up under the sheets.

Sometimes my mother's voice would call up the stairs, "George, finish the story now." But my father continued until it was the natural time to stop, and not before.

My father was a very private person. If I ever had occasion to go into his bedroom, I always knocked on the door. Sometimes my mother sent me up to wake him as he always worked shifts and would be in bed when I returned from school. I would peep round the door and he would say, "Tell your mother I'll be down."

I knew that once he came downstairs he would invariably take me out, if only round to his allotment where I would play on the swing, move planks of wood to rehouse and disturb the homes of insects, or check out the many hens my father kept. I would become Florence Nightingale for all poor animals but my father always made a point of telling me that nature must be left alone and that everything must inevitably return to the soil.

I strongly resisted this idea, saving sick hens, starving chickens and orphaned cats. I always had the large allotment for my 'hospital', much to my mother's relief. Here I would determinedly nurse sick creatures despite my father's insistence to leave things to nature. Inevitably it would be here where I cried when I was unsuccessful in saving the life of a chicken or injured hedgehog.

My father taught me to treasure certain times by acknowledging them in silence. Together we would sit on the bench amongst the vegetables on his allotment at such times and I learnt the value of silence. Occasionally he would take me into a church but never when there was a service. On these occasions he would be still, an unobtrusive and insignificant figure who would sit quietly and pray. He never preached religion to me but I learnt to honour and respect places of worship. He taught me a fierce independence, never treating me as a girl, but as an equal to any boy, instilling in me the belief that I must live with my own decisions.

As I grew older and moved away from home he would write to me, such words of hope and wisdom that I read his letters to this day. They are sustenance for my soul and I turn to them when I need to.
When we were out walking in Cheshire or Wales, he would often scribble a little poem, which I never saw and knew not to ask about, and hid it in a dry stonewall. I often wonder how many of those words of wisdom have since been discovered. In his last few years in his late sixties, he attended University. His death was so sudden that young students, attracted by his intellect, came to our home to enquire of his whereabouts. They broke down and cried upon hearing the news of his death.

Father, I miss you so much, from the moment when I can first remember curling up in your strong arms and pushing my cold little feet onto your warm chest, through the times of my growing up until that final goodbye in Crewe on an autumn day in 1977. It is only now that I understand your explanation when you refused the take the medication, which would have dulled your pain.

"No, I do not want it. I have known what it has been to live. Now I want to know what it is to die."

You calmed my soul, quickened my intellect and shared your love and understanding of life with those who could hear you.

My Mother, Edith James Madden (1901 – 1985)

EDITH ON THE BEACH

My mother locked the side gate by bolting it from the inside. She shut the front door and remained within her neat, well-furnished house, away from prying eyes. This occurred on many afternoons.

I never knew what she did during these times as I played out until dusk, visiting the Mill fields near our home and spending time at my grandmother's house a street away from our home.

My mother never shouted and yet she seemed to be silently screaming. She was tired and overworked; yet she did not work beyond the home. She was older than many mothers and I only remember her with white hair.

I remember her telling me that she had her teeth removed at the same time as my father's eldest sister, Evelyn, because false teeth were fashionable in those days. When I questioned further I never discovered exactly who this mysterious aunty Evelyn was or why I had never met her. It was a secret never disclosed to me in her lifetime.

My mother visited the hairdresser regularly. One day, while perming her thin white hair, the hairdresser accidentally burnt the top of her forehead. The long horizontal red mark stained her forehead until the day she died. For reasons I never understood she refused to complain about this accident, choosing to cover up the burn mark with powder. Despite this, my mother was a pretty woman.

She devoted her life to my sister and I. She was extremely ambitious for us, seeing education as a way to promote us beyond our working class peers. She was the driving force in our household and yet she only visited our school on parents' evening, borrowing a hat from her friend in Manor Way, a wealthier street around the corner from us. She was ambitious for our futures, believing fervently in education for girls.

I was embarrassed, as I always thought we had so much in material wealth and that there was no necessity for this. I never realized as a child that she was kept to a tight budget. My father explained that if we ran a car, then we must have a slightly less expensive house and this must have applied to other material things. We never had a phone as he laughed and said that it would give my mother ideas of grandeur! If she needed to use a telephone she walked around the corner to the telephone box. In emergencies she asked Mrs Chalwin, our next-door neighbour, for the favour.

From the age of three I was aware of a highly emotional and tense relationship between my mother and father. If there were rows, it was usually about her spending too much money on the house. Looking back I can see that she merely wanted to 'update' with more modern furnishings such as a fitted stair carpet and a one-tone carpet throughout the house. Strangely, after my father died, this was the first thing that she did but I think that it gave her no great joy. It was all too late. It was my father she missed now even though her home had been her life.

My mother was always looking for a peaceful existence, which was a paradox as she lived with a turbulent and passionate man. My father often explained to us, when we were little, that our mother wasn't very well. She lacked calcium and he had sought specialist advice for her. This helped to explain her silences and weariness.

But as a child I sensed many restrictions placed on my mother, including great secrecy about certain matters surrounding my mysterious aunt Evelyn.

What was the barrier between us when I was little? Certainly I could be a stubborn child and defied her often. She always put up with my determined ways and sometimes I wished that she would be openly angry with me. I loved my mother but felt that I never really knew her.

I recall coming home from the Mill fields with my sister. Our entire gang of friends were covered in mud, as it was a wet, wintry day. I wished that she would shout at us like the other mothers but we were greeted with a little smile and whisked out of our muddy clothes before we entered the warm neat living room.

'THE CREWE GANG'
Outside 100 Ernest St, Crewe. L-R: Janice, My sister, Anne Younger,
Terry Palin, Maureen and Sean Kenny plus Peter, our Sealyham dog

I never remember feeling jealousy towards anyone. I was perfectly happy in my own world. If I needed to escape, I simply ran to 35 Neville Street and confided in my Nanny or Aunty Cis. Nanny would brush aside any naughty thing I might have done and threaten what she would do to 'that George Madden' if he came looking for me. I always escaped on my own and my sister was left with my doting mother. I never questioned my mother's love for years because I was a happy child.

The first time that I became aware of conflict was at the home of my Aunty Winnie, one of my Mum's sisters. She was kind to me but one day I heard her say to my Aunty Cis that 'Our Edie ought to be ashamed of herself, making such a favourite' of my sister and excluding me. Hearing this remark puzzled me, but I wasn't upset.

No one realized that I wasn't excluded, as I didn't seek the same pleasures as my sister. Because of the situation as seen by adults, I had the exclusive love of my grandfather and the doting love of my grandmother and Aunty Cis. My mother made a point of telling me that I was 'Cissy's little pet', and so I was!

Then one day my mother made a silly remark, which deeply affected me for years. My sister and I had discovered a girl at school who was adopted and we questioned our mother on the significance of this. She turned to me and said, 'You are adopted.'

My heart nearly stopped beating as my mother and sister laughed at the joke. Uncertainties and dark fears rose within me. Everything in me proclaimed that it could not be true. I was, after all, a twin. My sister was there to prove it. But then, I didn't look like my sister and I'd often heard my mother say that my sister resembled her!

For weeks I convinced myself that they had chosen me to be a friend for their one child. I cried myself to sleep at night and couldn't talk to anyone about it. Finally, I confided in Nanny who took me into her parlour and told me the details of my birth. Later, I found my birth certificate and checked it against my sister's certificate.

From then on, I grew uncertain of my mother's feelings. Nothing about my physical appearance seemed to please her. My straight thick hair sprouted in all directions and could only be controlled by plaits, which I pulled out at every opportunity.

My strong, white, even teeth were compared to my father's teeth. My mother was at pains to tell me that my sister had her teeth, her hair, her skin and her nervous ways! We must all worry about her and preserve her against the harsh winds of reality.

I excelled in one area, which delighted my mother. Success at school brought a rare smile to her face. I am not sure whether my love of learning came from an urge to please her or whether it was innate.

I came to realise that my sister was the favourite child. So one day, at the age of thirteen, I told my mother so. She was hysterical, telling me not to be so silly. She loved me just as much but I could cope with life, I was stronger, I didn't have 'bad nerves' and I wasn't as thin as a stick!

And so it remained like that. An uneasy peace with my mother lasted throughout my adolescence. By my side, my sister rode the storms of growing up, anxiously watched over by my mother.

It came as quite a shock to my mother when one day, at the age of eighteen, I bought a black dress and had my hair cut into a fashionable style. I remember her remarking on my appearance to my father and saying that I looked 'quite pretty'.

My mother began to separate our lives quite deliberately, telling me one thing and my sister another. She always praised my strength of purpose but I sensed a fear in her regarding my determination. All my young life I had been given mental freedom and I was not about to relinquish it now.

This strained relationship remained between us for many years until the births of my three children. Then I began to understand my Mum and realized how incredible she had been when we were small girls. It must have been almost impossible at times to reconcile with the Madden secrets that she had vowed to keep. She was very much in love with my father and sought to give him the home he had lacked as a child.

Who really knows what goes on between two people? I was merely the child, an onlooker into their world, which I didn't understand. I had glimmerings of insight before my mother died. She loved my two girls but took on the second one as her very own. This beautiful baby turned out to be the one she really had desired, long blonde curls, exquisite and finely boned, a dolly to dress up; loving and devoted to her Nanny, she spent all her tiny days with her.

As my parents grew older the divisions between them were more sharply defined. With her dreams centred on her powerful husband, her only other life lay through her grandchildren. Some of the happiest times I ever spent were at Holyhead when Mum and aunty Cis travelled by train to spend many holidays with us.

My children continued their strong relationship with their grandmother and aunt in this way, meeting them at the railway station, overwhelming them with hugs and kisses. The bond deepened between them and I recall wonderful times spent in our Welsh home.

My father wrote letters to Mum, even though she was away for only a few days, which was very comforting to her. Meanwhile Cissy was continuing to do all the outrageous things that had endeared her to me when I was a child. She had acquired a 'boyfriend' who often came with them on the holidays. He was made welcome too, so we all thrived within this extended family.

My mother's favourite grandchild burst into the kitchen one day, her tiny blond curls untidily escaping from her plaits, large grey eyes showing concern. "Mum, guess what? Nanny is on the grass green by the beach and she is rolly pollying down the grass with us. She's amazing!"

When we reached the grass green all we could see was my mother and eldest daughter sitting on a seat at the top of the hill, both innocently licking ice creams. It was their secret and nothing was ever said. My mother was almost into her eighties at that time!

After my father's death my mother deteriorated in mental health.

She became depressed, longing for those happy times when she had the security and love of the man who had been her mate for all those years. Her life lacked purpose.

Finally she decided not to eat and in a very anxious state of mind she was admitted to hospital where she was fed on a drip. I traveled from Cornwall to see her and was shocked to find her looking so thin and tiny. Outraged I shouted at her, wanting to recall her even though I knew it was useless. "Mum, why are you not eating? Why do you want to die?"

She smiled a slow sad smile. "Last night I had a dream. I dreamed about when you were a little girl, but oh so determined." Her voice trailed away. "We were all so happy. We had such lovely times. I dreamed about your father." Her voice faltered and her mouth closed in a tight refusal to say mo more.

Two days later she died at the hospital. When I returned to the family home it was to discover that everything was neatly in order. There was no rubbish to throw away, no tidying up or sorting out. She had meticulously prepared her exit from this world.

My Grandmother, Edith James (1874 – 1965)

As a small child, my physical contact with other human beings was lifeblood to me. Growing up with a twin sister meant that I was never alone, but from long beyond my earliest memories the warmth of human contact was an integral part of my soul.

When we were tiny children, we would both wait for my father to come in from work. Once he was washed and changed, he settled in the large brown leather armchair and we would climb immediately onto his strong lap and cuddle against his broad chest; one small girl held in each arm, we would press against his face, leaning against him, secure within his arms. I can recall his heart beating strongly. We put little hands near to his face and he would snap at us imitating a crocodile and making us squeal with delight.

Janice, Father, My Sister, My Cousin

In contrast, I can only remember coldness from my mother in those childhood days. Of course there was concern and love but nothing physical. She used to say to me, "We've never been a kissing family, have we?" Then she would laugh nervously. She often expressed the belief that kissing involved germs, reassuring herself that this was the real reason for not being able to express her feelings. We would have little pecks on our cheeks but they felt meaningless.

My other home was, of course, at my grandmother's house and as soon as I could walk, I would be there, within the comfort of a home where food and love were given out in equal abundance. My grandmother loved me devotedly and I basked in that knowledge. Once I entered the yard, the back gate would be locked and I became the only child to be doted upon by a grandmother who was wise, ageless and unquestioning in her love.

She was a tiny woman, who had been brought up in a large Victorian family. Her mother, Abigail Longland, had been one of the few educated women in the nearby village of Shavington and wrote letters for the many illiterate villagers. Her sister had been in service to Queen Victoria, working in the royal nursery and my grandmother, along with her brothers and sisters, had received several 'hand downs', (clothes) from the Royal household.

I liked nothing more than to encourage my grandmother, whom I always called 'Nanny', to relate experiences of her own early childhood. I recall tales of basic education in the schoolroom, which housed all ages. My grandmother adored the young teacher who struggled to educate her class of sixty, while at the same time coughing up blood, the telltale sign of tuberculosis.

My grandmother, being the favourite in the class, volunteered to wash the blood covered rags, carrying out the bucket which had been placed by the teacher's desk, and hanging the rags out to dry. She felt honoured to be asked to do this small chore and when the young teacher finally died of TB, Edith James left school, at the age of only nine.

Her stories carried me back into a world where the working class of England struggled to exist despite extreme poverty and disease. Born in 1874, only four years after the death of Charles Dickens, she had survived and even thrived against a social background that was daunting.

NANNY

She recalled those early Dickensian stories, set out in penny papers for all to read if they were able, but expressed no great shock or dismay over the abysmal social conditions for the working class of that day. She put her head down and survived.

Nanny was a hard woman, practical and traditional in her outlook. She shocked my sister and I one day when we discovered a tiny mouse in her neat shed. We called her out to look at it and swiftly seizing a broom, she beat it to death. This was the only time that I witnessed such cruelty; my grandmother was certainly no lateral thinker or dreamer!

Life was hard but logical. She had swept dark shadows away long ago and never showed weakness. She was proud, tough and completely predictable. Doubt and uncertainty never haunted her. Her children were her life and in this respect I feel that I may have inherited this same quality. Why she loved me with such devotion I will never really understand, but it gave me great strength during my childhood years

I was allowed untold license regarding the cupboard under the stairs where the button box lived. I spent hours looking through all the stored treasures and Nanny would often stop her endless chores to explain the origin of the buttons. Every one of them had a life history!

One day, as I sat beside her on her couch, she told me about her first born son, William, whose photo hung in the kitchen for daily viewing. The photograph showed a handsome man, forever young. Nanny told me many times about the 1914-1918 war that took him from her, her beloved first-born child with such poor eyesight that he could hardly see to read. We went into the front room and there, in the gloom behind the netted curtains, she would unfold his uniform of death. We would look at the jacket and she would turn it over to reveal the bayonet hole and the dried blood. I imagined poor William stumbling across the trenches before inevitably receiving the fatal wound in his back.
My grandma and I stood silently, in remembrance of her favourite child and I wondered at the cruelty of the returned uniform that gave her such comfort. Then, wordlessly, it was folded, preserved once again in tissue paper and disappeared into the back of a cupboard.

Later in my life, my grandmother told me about her trip to France, a journey that had taken her away from English soil for the first and only time. She recalled fields of poppies, William's small patch of earth at the Somme and a hellish sea journey in keeping with the entire miserable farewell that she had to take.

My grandmother continued to bake and cook for a family of nine, quite regardless of the fact that only she and her divorced daughter remained. Her cooking was wonderful. We had our dinners at 35 Neville Street, Crewe, until we were seventeen. It was an odd arrangement that was never questioned. My mother and aunty also ate dinner with us and washed the dishes afterwards.

Dinners were cooked on a black stove fuelled by coal. Preparation began at dawn every day and by eight o'clock in the morning, apples would be stewing, meat slowly roasting and vegetables awaiting their fate on the hot stove.
My sister and I were sent out to play but we usually ate such vast quantities of food that we took turns to lie about on the famous couch until we could summon up sufficient energy to return to school. This chaise longue was positioned next to the door under the stairs. Nanny's daily ritual was to sleep on it every afternoon, despite the horse-hair filling which made it as hard as iron!

By eight each morning my grandmother, spotlessly clean and wrapped in a snow-white apron, would be plunging her hands into a yellow baking bowl, making delicious pastry. Everything was measured by experience; there were no scales in the house. The large wooden table was scrubbed and spotless to be later anointed with a starched white cloth and laid for dinner.

Once a week, a cart would deliver Stones' ginger ale and two bottles of pop - one Tizer and one Orangeade. My grandmother allowed us tiny glasses of our own choice to complement the delicious food.

The buying of the Sunday joint was also a ritual. My mother contributed towards the cost. Early every Saturday morning my grandmother dressed in her best white blouse, always fastened at the neckline by a pretty brooch. She wore her woollen coat and a fine hat and set out for Nantwich Road, Crewe for the meat, which was selected with great care and expertise.

Later, it was washed, soaked in vinegar, placed on a large plate and left in the bath where it remained, secluded and cool until Sunday morning. Of course there was no fridge and the downstairs bathroom was the coldest room in the house!

Much detailed discussion would take place during and after this weekly expedition, which I was often privileged to join. Nanny met old friends along the streets and they would exchange family news before they said goodbye. Nanny wasn't a gossip but this network of friends provided her with her only social life and it was sufficient to sustain her until the following week.

She often included glowing references of my sister and I in the conversation and we listened happily before skipping ahead of her, each clutching the pocket money that she had given to us. Her shopping route never varied.

She travelled on the same pavements, crossed at the same points on the roads and purchased her goods at the same shops.

Occasionally, we ventured into the heart of Crewe on the bus to visit a grocer at the other side of town. His name was Ernie Salisbury and it was here that my grandmother bought her flour and sugar from large sacks. Butter was cut from a huge yellow mound resting on the counter.

We always called at the Co-op on Gresty Road where we watched in delight as the assistant sent the money hurtling along the wire contained in a small brass cup. At the office, change and the divvy slip were returned by the wire cable. This was known as the flying fox. Divvy numbers meant receiving a refund at Christmas time, the savings being paid into a Club to help buy festive treats. Our divvy number was 19019.

Our Christmas meal was served grandly on the carved oak table in my grandmother's front room that was opened up for the occasion. A small token fire burnt in the grate and the curtains were drawn back to let in the weak winter light. My father never ate at my Grandmother's home as he worked every Christmas time for as long as I can remember. This was by choice.

We carried up our toy sacks that we discovered when we woke on Christmas morning. By 11 o'clock on Christmas day we arrived at my granmother's home where we once again enjoyed our presents with Nanny and Aunty Cis.

During my early years, the stern figure of my grandfather moved quietly about the house. His lilting Welsh voice and gentle manner told of a man who had long since been dominated by his wife, but there was steeliness in his cold, ice blue eyes, which belied this subordination. His role in family life seemed secondary and compared with my Nanny he was a shadowy figure. His daily ritual was to dart about the house with a tightly rolled up newspaper, which administered certain death to every fly. His aim was deadly accurate!

Very occasionally, I witnessed the vehemence in him. In his youth he had trained as a Baptist Minister and his silences were filled by unspoken thoughts. Even as he slept beneath a spread out newspaper, we were aware of his unbending attitudes. We longed to play jokes and poke the paper as it rose and fell with his breathing but we would never dare to do such a thing. We could not imagine the outcome!

He adored me and only I was allowed to sit on his chair. No explanation or compromise was permitted, as my sister discovered to her cost when she dared to take my place one day. My grandfather snatched her from the chair and declared that he was happy to allow her to eat dinners at his home but that was as far as it went!

I learnt of his death from a girl we hardly knew when we were returning from school one lunch hour for our dinner. Swinging on her front gate she was waiting for us to pass her house and as we did so she yelled out, "Your granddad is dead!" and triumphantly marched inside.

We raced up the street in disbelief only to find the front room curtains closed. Our dinners were out on the table but the house was very still and quiet. We continued to go there every day and I have no memory of his funeral.

Much later in our lives, we learnt of his agonizing illness and the incredible nursing by my grandmother who fought the stomach cancer that eventually killed him. He died in the front room where I was born and I missed him. That such nursing continued during all our visits without a disruption to our lives is a source of amazement to me. He was rarely spoken about from then on but occasionally when Nanny and I were alone she would smile gently, confiding in me that he had been a good man and a gentle father to her children.

Following his death I sat in his chair next to the wireless and struggled to remember this cold, uncommunicative man, the mate of my grandmother for so many years. My mother, who responded to his quiet and authoritarian manner, sadly missed his presence. My grandmother was far too brisk and dominant for my mother, who could not understand or cope with the strict social guidelines that she lived by.

My grandmother did not seek up to date furnishings or buy small nick knacks for the house. Cleanliness, hard work and preservation of family life provided her with a driving force that fed her purposeful daily routine. During the many years of visits to her home I never saw anything replaced. Frozen in time, the old wooden furniture remained in the same position throughout her life, polished and scrubbed until it shone.

As she approached her ninetieth year, my grandmother's only concession to her advanced years was to joke that she was ready for the workhouse and that she was 'an ugly old thing'. Age certainly didn't slow her down but slowly the shopping trips ceased. She rarely left her home, each day waiting for Cissy to return from work. The cooking stopped when I was seventeen; the fire died out and was eventually replaced by a small cooker that sat next to the sink. As she grew older and no longer felt required to cook for the family, my grandmother fell into an easy routine of living. She prepared small meals for herself, rarely cooked and slept on her couch every afternoon. Aunty Cissy cared for her even more attentively, placing no restrictions upon her whatsoever.

When I was very young I acquired an animal that became my closest friend. I named him Ernest and chose him from a family of rabbits bred in the backyard of a girl named Janice Brookshaw.

Although my mother had forbidden me to have a rabbit, my sister and I defied her and went to the Brookshaw house to inspect the animals. My sister chose a black and white Dutch rabbit and I opened the cage to discover several beautiful baby grey Chinchillas. The boldest one tumbled out onto my hands and I claimed him immediately, naming him Ernest after our street.

Jan and Ernest 1953

Later, he was to acquire a number of names; Oliver after the owner of the local shop; Cecil after an uncle, Winston after the Prime Minister, Percival after another uncle and James after my grandparents. His final name was Madden Esq!

Our pets had to live in my grandmother's garden as my mother refused to have any animals. The arrangement was convenient as I could feed my rabbit every lunch hour. My sister named her rabbit Beauty and I cannot recall its fate.

But I well remember Ernest. He became an amazing character, adored by both my grandmother and myself. She would toast bread in her oven for him and talk to him during the summer months when she sat outside in the garden, shelling the peas or crocheting. My father built him a splendid hutch, which stood high in the air on tall wooden legs. Inside, he could jump up into a bedroom packed with hay.

I would tell Ernest all my secrets and he always understood. Quite often he was bad-tempered and would make an alarming growling sound, but I carried him around the wild garden and soothed his nerves by allowing him total freedom.

Here I let him loose to watch him for hours as he ran through the tall grass, jumping high in the air and banging his legs together! Strangely he acted like a wild creature and I was never sure if he would return from the tall grasses. But he always did!

Suddenly myxomotosis was heard of in the media. People out walking in the Cheshire countryside came across stumbling, blinded rabbits. Grotesque in their dying movements they crawled across the roads, crashed into trees and lay in the fields quivering until merciful death relieved the pain of their disease ridden bodies. The smell from their rotting flesh was awful and the sight of one near to Beeston Castle sent a chill through me.

I questioned my father on the possibility of Ernest catching 'myxi' but he reassured me that this would not happen. Ernest was isolated in my Nanny's garden and this was some kind of quarantine for him. Nevertheless I was watchful for months. Little did any of us know then that an introduced flea caused the terrible disease and that the fresh hay from the cattle market pens would bring death to my rabbit. I studied the effects of the disease and knew all the signs of early onset; drooping ears, listlessness, shaking head and trembling. The ears would flop with no control, eyes would swell and then the head until the rabbit became disfigured and blind.

I would sit Ernest on my knee and tell him the fate of his wild cousins. His soft velvet ears would twitch and turn as he listened to me. As I talked about my plans for the future that included being a writer, I would part his fur, blowing softly into it to check for anything unusual.

On platform two of Crewe Railway Station was a machine that stamped out metal names. One day I went there to make a name for his hutch, carrying home the long metal tag with the seven names. I remember nailing it onto his hutch door and as I hammered it onto the wood I felt that this would give him an identity, which would protect him.

But then came the dreadful lunch hour in May. I can still remember the flowers and blossoms as I ran home to my grandmother's house, calling his name as I charged around the corner to his hutch. Suddenly I stopped. I did not hear the customary thump of his large body as he descended from his bedroom. I remember drawing in my breath, willing myself to kneel down and peer through the wire. His ears were flopping over dull eyes! I knew immediately that he had the disease. I screamed in anger, flying past the open door of the house where my dinner was already laid out. I rushed down the street to find my father who was returning from his allotment.

"You," I screamed. "You were wrong! Ernest is dying because of you. You wouldn't let me get him injected for the disease and now he is dying."

My father was shocked. I recall him standing very still as I screamed at him.

"Don't say anything, I hate you, I hate you, you are a murderer," I screamed and I kicked him very hard on his leg.

I remember little more about that day except that at school we had running and I cried for hours, firstly around the perimeter of the playing fields, then in the classroom and finally all the way home. My mother was silent, even my sister was lost for words, but I saved my silent anger for my father. I refused to speak to him.

The following lunch hour I made the dreaded journey up the street and in through the back gate. My Nanny put her arms around me and I wept. Then I walked slowly round the side of the shed. I gasped with astonishment. Everything had gone! The hutch, the paving stone on which it had stood, the bits of straw which had spilled out of the door when he jumped out for his daily run, everything! He simply ceased to exist!

I never asked about him ever again. No one spoke of him either. It was a code of silence, which was never broken until my father was dying. Then he told me. Ernest was buried at the end of his allotment. He was never made to suffer the full effects of the terrible man made disease. Later on television I would see news items from Australia showing thousands of dying rabbits stumbling towards water holes and I felt incredible anger towards 'progress'.

My Nanny showed great compassion towards me and all over a rabbit! She, who had hammered a mouse to death, visited the grave of her first born son, nursed her husband until his death and reared six children, revealed such love and care towards me. I can never recall words being spoken but from then on I would go to her house for afternoon tea and the gate would be locked behind me!

Tea was a very different affair, being more genteel than the family dinners. A lace cloth covered the scrubbed wooden table, small sandwiches and cake came from the pantry, sweet condensed milk was used in the tea and I was allowed to lick the spoon. Here we sat, just the two of us and quietly we would simply enjoy each other's company. We laughed about Cissy's lipstick which

Nanny called 'lip stitch'. We looked at the button box together and stories of the last century were told. It was a healing time for me.

That was the only time that I heard her verbally criticize my mother. "She's a strange one, your mother. Sometimes I can't understand her." And she used to shake her head disapprovingly. I felt puzzled as I wondered why she even expected my mother to mourn a dead rabbit!

On occasional weekends, I would return home from College but my first port of call, as I walked home from the railway station, would be my grandmother's house. As she grew weaker, there were rare occasions when she was persuaded to rest in bed until noon. Leaving my suitcase at the bottom of the stairs, I'd climb into her big bed and we'd lie and talk together before I finally went home.

One bitterly cold winter's day, my grandmother struggled down the path to brush away the snow. Streets were made accessible in this way and neighbours cast disapproving glances at patches of snow that were not cleared. Sadly, my grandmother caught pneumonia as a direct result of the cold. We all visited her as she lay dying, and I was angry with disbelief. Already caught up in the beginnings of a desperately unhappy marriage, my strong bond with Nanny sustained and comforted me.

On the day of her funeral I refused to go. I lay in bed for twenty-four sad hours with the sheets pulled over my head. I was twenty-five years old, my grandmother was ninety-one and I felt as though I had lost my best friend.

My Aunt, Phyllis James Calderbank (1905 - 1985)

Being a twin was inevitably more complicated for my mother, who was already in her mid forties when my sister and I began to stray beyond the confines of our home and immediate environment.

Mother, always hopeful for a family of one neat, submissive child, received a contradictory answer in the shape of two non-identical girls who were to challenge, worry and exhaust her until the day she died!

When we were born, on September 14th 1940, in the front room of the parlour of my grandmother's house, 35 Neville Street, Crewe, it was into a Europe seething with war.

Our mother, at thirty-nine years of age, gave birth to us with the aid of a midwife and my grandmother. We were identical weights at birth, a remarkable fact which was recorded in the Lancet medical journal. I was born twenty minutes before my sister, who posed a problem - arriving feet first.

I have since pondered on that strange fact. She must have been standing on me in our mother's womb or had she wrapped her little arms around me? Did she assist in my birth, launching me into a world that has intrigued me ever since? Or was she thoroughly disgusted with the lack of space?

So I was born, followed by my sister, into a room heavy with Victorian furniture, large Baptist Bibles and a sideboard so ornate and intricate that just to look at it was confusing. No doubt our family heirlooms on my mother's side were covered with dustsheets and the room prepared for the imminent birth, watched over by the portrait of our Great Grandmother, Abigail Longland.

We arrived in the darkness of early morning, safe and loved as, across the channel, other twins were sacrificed on the Nazi altar or experimented upon. How fortunate we were.

Our father carried death from the north to the south of the country on his steam train packed with explosives. Thus the balance was completed and one dark haired baby and her bald headed sister were swaddled and placed in a large cardboard box, which fitted into the enclosed space under the stairs. Here, alongside our overwhelmed mother, resilient grandmother and, intermittently, our Aunty Cis, we sheltered from the horror of the bombing.

What could our mother do with two babies? She found an easy solution. Mentally, she gave one away and it remained like that until the day she died. She bonded with my sister and gave me to my Aunty Cis, who was childless. My aunty told me, as I grew older, that she was given a choice and selected me because I had thick straight black hair which reminded her of her own hair. Cissy also claimed me as 'the best baby', setting up rivalry between my sister and I that has been difficult to understand ever since. We grew up in our own home with constant help and mothering from our grandmother and aunty, who always declared me 'her own'.

As we became older, we quickly responded to the lively nature of Cissy. She appeared to be a generation younger than my mother, who quickly resumed her former responsibilities, carrying out a routine designed for a childless couple.

Our home remained neat, clean and expensively furnished - our other home was associated with lavish meals, love, exploration and curiosity.

My grandmother's button box, the dark secrets of the cupboard under the stairs and the long, rambling garden that obstinately repelled cultivation provided us with endless exploration.

Cissy joined in with us in all our exploits. She knelt by the pond beyond the garden, jar in hand, as she captured tadpoles. She climbed into the hawthorn hedges, scrambling for birds' eggs and lifted us up one by one to peer at the baby birds. We revelled in her company. She introduced us to lipstick and even the occasional puff of one of her many cigarettes. She spent her wages on us, trailing to Manchester on shopping expeditions.

In return, we drowned her with love, kissing and hugging her until she squealed with delight. She was our sister, our passionate introduction to a world of uninhibited communication. This appeared to have little connection with formal education in the form of school, which was fast approaching!

While we began to discover formal learning and the disciplines of school, Cissy worked first at the railway canteen and later as a cook for the local hospital. We always wondered about this, as she could not cook! My grandmother was the expert who prepared our midday dinner every day, apart from Saturdays, until we were seventeen! However, our aunty was a cook by name and cycled some considerable distance to work every day until her retirement from the hospital at sixty.

As we grew older, we discovered that she had been married for a very brief time, at first happily but later she was betrayed and hurt. She had crept home to live with her mother and never left again.

She gave my grandmother her independence unquestioningly, popping most of her wages into her mother's large black bag every Saturday morning. Her sisters, including my mother, betrayed her loyalty with stories that hinted of secret liaisons and clandestine affairs with men. The word 'sex' hovered in the air but was only hinted at in veiled conversations. There was a strong sense of disapproval within the family and a suggestion of men friends who were not considered suitable.

Of course, all of this made her even more attractive to my sister and I. How could there be anything wicked about a pretty aunty who tucked her dress into her knickers on Rhyl beach and ran into the sea up to her waist? How could a young woman who was brave enough to pull the skeletons out of the family cupboard and give them a good shake every now and then possibly affect us adversely?

Certainly my father could find several of these excellent qualities in our aunty as he mended her bicycle for work, invested her money in shares which brought her a lifetime wage, and gently and kindly told her off for smoking.

When she was a small child, Cissy had surrendered all her hopes of a better life to her sisters. She was no doubt the Cinderella of the family and certainly the prettiest one. I remember her laughingly telling us a story of my grandmother making her a little dress from the cloth of a black umbrella for her first school clothes, as all available money had gone on the other children.

Cissy was also a twin, an amazing fact, as she never seemed close to her twin brother, Philip. Brooding and clever, an undiscovered mathematical genius, he took to wandering away from home in early manhood and caused the family great distress. He later married and had one son. We were entertained every Sunday by his scientific puzzles and bizarre and convincing ghost stories, but I never saw Cissy display any outward sign of love towards him.

Adored and fretted over by my grandmother, he never replaced his beloved eldest brother William, who died in the First World War at the age of eighteen. Wonderful memories of William were recalled by all four sisters. Brother Philip was seen as spoilt, which suggested love channelled in his direction as the only son, following the death of his brother.

Cissy was always tolerant of him but not close. She challenged and irritated him with her lively ways and endless energy. I could well imagine their volatile child relationship - he, studious and at heart an academic - Cissy, singing, laughing and thumbing her nose to all authority.

As I grew older, I became very close to my aunty. I found within her a great wisdom and kindness that I could not find in my mother. We formed a ritual in my childhood that lasted until she died. It started when my sister and I could walk. We would visit my grandmother's house and be allowed to return down the street on our own. My aunty would stand at the gate, shouting, waving and blowing kisses until we reached our own gate, in a street that could be seen by my aunty. On darkening evenings we hurried quickly past the silent houses. Very few front rooms were lit up, as they were the parlours used only for special occasions such as Christmas and funeral farewells. Every time we looked back, there she stood, waving. This ritual carried on long after our grandmother's death and continued with my own children until the day came when Cissy could no longer walk to the gate because of illness.

When my grandmother died, controversy raged between two of the sisters concerning the ownership of the house. This disagreement was aggravated even further when my aunt invited an older man friend to share the last six years of her life.

Anxious that the family home might be left to him, they humiliated themselves over the grave of my dead poor aunty by angrily proclaiming ownership of the property. My mother did not include herself in this disgraceful and final putting down of our beloved aunty, for which I am grateful.

Cissy never spoke of affairs of the heart and I was deeply saddened to think that she had never been loved. In today's society she would have blossomed; an alternative spirit who could adapt easily to almost any situation. She was a woman of the late twentieth century trapped in a disapproving society, a remnant of the Victorian age.

Now, as I look back, I can see that she gave my grandmother security, dignity and love until she was ninety-one years old. It was she who was so instrumental in our bringing up, showing us physical love and affection. She was our guardian angel in so many ways.

After her death, I helped to clean out the ornate sideboard in her front room and amongst the many little letters and photographs from my sister and I, which she had kept and treasured, I discovered an answer to my mourning.

Now the lovers are long dead and gone I can print the letter as a celebration of my love for my 'mother'. Someone, somewhere had indeed recognised this very special human being and loved her with all his mind and body.

AUNTY CIS AND CISSY'S LOVER

Thursday 30th Sept.
10.30 a. m.

My Dear Love,

Once again I am with you alone. and this is another day without news about and from my Darling. Are you really so busy? Well I guess and understand. I do nevertheless hope you are always well and happy and not making yourself overtired.

As regards myself, my Sweet Own Phyl, I am always busy actually and that work and strain at getting hold of a job keeps very much hold of my mind. This does not mean in the least that I am forgetting my Darling. How could I with such a background and frame of love happiness and joys she has given me. How often I still think and remind of the happy hours we have lived and loved together.

The sweetness of your kisses, the warmth of your body, the beat of your haert, the ~~warmth~~ fire of your love are still in me and I still enjoy all that which you so generously and without reserve haven given me, yourself whole haert and body, soul and mind. Yes, my Darling, we have had a wonderfull time of love. and that is unforgettable. You are such a wonderful love and so full of sweetness. You have conquered me all and I have given myself wholy to you and ~~will remain such~~ for always. How I do wish you were here with me right now in this parc where I am writing and telling you about my love. How I would love to tell you the words of love that burn my lips and hold you in my arms and feel the beating of your haert, and the sweetness of your kisses, the yielding of your body and abandonement of your whole self to my love. Would we be happy!

Well, now, my Dearest Love, I must finish this but not without telling you how much I am longing for news from you about yourself and telling me about your love, wishes, longings and most intimate desires and thoughts.

I so much do want to participate in your whole and most intimate life.

And now I say Cheerio Darling. Take good care of yourself for our love's sake and be happy and cheerful. I am and remain yours for ever and my love is you and yours.

Paul.

x x x x x x x x x x x

Chapter Two:

Friends and Lovers 1953 - 1960

Shendy

The Mill Stream 1953

The mill fields were a paradise for all young people who lived at our end of Crewe town. Within a walking distance of two streets and an allotment, we would reach a virtually untouched countryside that offered us adventures and total freedom. My sister and I would walk down the cinder track, past the council houses and on towards a small farm which lay in a hollow. Beyond, lay the shunting yards and Rope Lane.

Within these boundaries lay several fields, a wood and wreathing paths, which eventually led to an old mill, surrounded by a huge pond, the surface of which remained glass-like, even when two swans crossed it. The greasy waters of this mysterious place hid such dark secrets that we never ventured near. It was a passing place and even on a sunny day I sensed the dark powers and treachery below its calm surface and hurried on. There was a ghastly rumour that was told of small children running from that big house, playing by the side of the millpond and watched over by their nanny. They slipped and fell, sinking below its murky waters. The nanny tried to retrieve them. Days later the bodies were found, wrapped deep in the arms of the weeds and they were brought to the surface and laid upon the banks, death clutching death, the children in the arms of their nanny.

The path led over a wooden bridge below which water tumbled into a weir. Beyond the bridge lay the old mill and then the busyness of the main road where the silence unfolded abruptly. We rarely entered the mill fields this way, choosing the cinder path that led us forward and home again. Unspoken law between us dictated that we never ventured beyond the wood itself. I cannot recall ever not going to this magical place. I always seemed to know of it. All the young people met over there to light fires, swing on thick-knotted ropes, make dens and pick flowers. From the council and private houses, young people would automatically head in its direction, drawn by a strange magical spell into this other world where grown-ups were vanquished.

Here we played, laughed, talked, planned and dreamed, finding total freedom. Grammar school pupils, who were later to become scientists and writers, would go hand in hand with friends from homes that bulged with fifteen children. It was Utopia and it did exist, as my sister and I were there to witness it. We knew everyone and they knew us. A stranger would have been spotted immediately.

So it was that one spring day, when the stream, which ran the full length of the mill fields to feed directly into the dark pond, was in flood, a strange small boy was spotted in the first field beyond the farm. We gathered round to watch him approach us, a gang of twenty young people between the ages of ten to eighteen. On he came, walking confidently through the tall spring grass. His appearance was amazing and in total contrast to anyone there. We were clad in gabardine macs and wellingtons, steam rising from our breath, as the day was icy and damp.

The stranger stood on the other side of the pipe, which provided daring crossings for those who were brave enough. He was small, my shoulder height, and was dressed in a dirty white jacket smeared with suspicious stains. His black, greasy, man's trousers were wide and baggy, having been well worn and then handed on and cut down to size and his thin white legs disappeared inside black wellingtons. He smiled confidently at us and a lock of dull untrimmed black hair fell over his left eye. Automatically shaking it back, he revealed a white face and dark, deep set eyes.

He was a comic sight standing on the bank and everyone laughed. Amazingly, he laughed back. Then he sprang forward and, with incredible agility, ran across the wet pipe. Below, the stream was in full flood and very few of us had ventured near to its treacherous slopes that morning, fearing the deep watery holes and banks that were continually breaking up and being swept away within seconds. We all had an unspoken fear of the millpond and the weir. Now, here was this comic boy, vanquishing all dark thoughts by walking across the pipe as if it was part of the path! On he came up the bank, until he stood before us in the dirty white coat, which appeared to be casually worn over a greasy black jacket, the upper part of the man's suit

"What's your name?" someone enquired, and with a broad smile that revealed a chipped tooth, he replied "Shendy" and promptly bent forward and walked up the bank on his hands! We stared in wonder at this small, pale boy who performed like a circus clown at his own initiation ceremony, which would allow him to become one of us. As he walked his hands up the bank, the wide trouser legs gaped open revealing a white bottom. He had no underpants on! No one said anything; indeed they were far too impressed by this strange new boy. He arrived like a bright beam of sunshine and by the end of the morning he was part of our gang.

Flinging himself onto the knotted rope, he sailed with great agility over the raging stream and back again. Tarzan himself could not compete! We were impressed. We discovered that the family had recently moved from the other end of Crewe into a house in Gresty Road. Later, he would tell us that he was from a family of seventeen. He had seven brothers and seven sisters, all alive and well, and a mother and father.

No one questioned these facts. A number of children came from large families and knew the face of poverty. The baggy trousers were 'cut downs' from his brother Arthur, who was the eldest in the family. The white coat was part of his butcher's uniform. At the age of ten, he was working practically full time, assisting the butcher in his bloody chores. School rested uneasily, somewhere vague between work and sleep. Shendy became part of the mill fields, along with the Garretts, Peter Armstrong, Norman Skellen, the Podmores, the Sims and the Madden twins.

After school, we would rush over there, enjoying the light nights of the summer months. As we had 'failed' the 11+, we were blessed with very little homework and total freedom. However, our ambitious mother still pursued future pathways to the Grammar School and education remained a priority in our house. Shendy would tell us amazing stories of his school life, without bitterness or regret.

I remember asking him if he stayed for school dinners and he recalled the one humiliating time when his mother had managed to find the money for him. Excited and proud to be with the others in the dining room on this cold winter day, he had been spotted by the teacher on duty and made to stand on a chair because he had a runny nose. She screamed at him to get his handkerchief and he jumped down in shame and ran home. In a family of fifteen, such a thing as a handkerchief was not heard of – sleeves had to make do!

As the next four years passed, Shendy and I became good friends. He made us all laugh and yet he was sensitive and perceptive. Unlike my agile sister, I could not walk the pipe or swing across the stream. The boy in the cutdown suit reached out across the pipe and held my hand, guiding me over and at the same time laughing gently because of my fear. Looking back, I should have realised that his knowledge of women was vast; within a household of seven sisters and a loving and loving devoted mother; he must have been immersed in feminine love!

Sometimes I used to walk to the meat shop to wait for him and peep under the blinds to catch glimpses of his small quick body moving about amid the meat carcasses. He would wave and mouth a time when he would be out or shake his head when he knew that the job would go beyond midnight. The blinds were down so that he would not be caught working under age. Then I realised that his house was only a short distance from the shop and occasionally I would knock on his door. Sometimes one of his handsome brothers would answer, or his father, dark eyed and thoughtful, would stand on the step, waiting, and I would run away, shy of this other world, so different from my own. I would catch glimpses of a hallway covered by newspapers laid down on the newly washed tiles, to be pulled up at the last minute when Shendy's mother returned from work. For work she did, cooking at a big house in Alsager and bringing home treats for her huge family. His father, injured in the Second World War, would cook and clean, very much the head of a household of thriving young men and women. Shendy was the last child and poorest one, fifteenth in line for necessities, which were hard to come by.

In the street near to his house were parked shining Velocette motorbikes, powerful machines with names such as Matchless, AJS, BSA and Ariel, evidence of his many brothers' ability to provide such luxuries through bricklaying and plumbing. We would brush past these silver giants, Shendy pointing out each one's identity. Occasionally I would spot one, roaring swiftly along Gresty Road, carrying a proud young man and his headscarfed girlfriend clinging possessively to his back. Shendy told me that one day he would own one too, but for years he helped to keep his parents and the remaining family instead.

Then he began to call at our house. Always he knocked on the front door to ask if I was in and was I going over to the mill? My mother, horrified by the dirty little figure, invariably in his butcher's jacket, would make a hurried excuse and close the door quickly. My sister and I would then rush round from the back gate to greet him, aware but indifferent to the smell of dead flesh that came from him. Off we would go to our place of sanctuary, Shendy always pushing an old bike worthy of a place in a museum. Sometimes and Alsatian/Labrador cross would follow him obediently, gazing at him with loving eyes. Once we reached the edge of the fields, Shendy would prop his bike up, vault over the barbed wire and somersault in the grass, making us laugh.

He was extremely daring. In one field ran four black horses. Swiftly they would join forces with each other, moving like liquid across the field. They were wild, being only occasionally ridden in the summer months. If bread were offered, they would approach calmly, tricking us into security by pushing their soft mouths into our hands for the bread. Then they would rear up and plunge backwards. They had bitten several people and our gang never ventured into their field.

Shendy told us stories of how he and his brothers could ride horses. They had close contact with the gypsies and even owned a horse of their own when they lived in the house at the other end of Crewe. One day he whistled to the four horses that reared and pranced behind the fence. My sister and I were terrified, begging him to remain with us, but laughingly he slipped beneath the wire and moved silently to the side of the black stallion, talking softly to it and stroking its winter mane. In a second he was astride its slippery back then the four horses were gone over the hill with our little white-coated friend with them. My sister and I looked at each other with dismay but soon we heard the thundering of hooves and back they came, steaming and charging, stopping within an inch of the sharp wire. Shendy slipped quietly from the stallion's back, gave one shrill whistle and they were gone again.

On more than one occasion we put him to the test, challenging his bravery. One Sunday afternoon we offered him our entire pocket money, a total of one shilling and ninepence, if he would jump off the bridge into the stream below. What started as a joke became a fearful reality as, taking up our offer immediately, he climbed precariously onto the bridge, and arms outstretched and walked the full length. We shut our eyes in horror and when we opened them he was gone! We ran shouting to peer down into the water, only to see him laughingly climbing up the bank, his dark eyes shining and his hand outstretched for the money.

One day, in the month of June when he was thirteen years old, Shendy called at 100 Ernest Street with a huge bunch of wild flowers for me.   My mother relented, allowing him into the living room to wait for us. I could sense her embarrassment when he handed me the flowers, then proceeded to roll about on her Wilton carpet like a dog! After satisfying himself of the reality of this luxury, he sat up in delight, explaining that he had never seen such a wonderful carpet.   There was no such thing in his house.   His mother and sisters made pegged rugs from strips of coloured material and these, along with cracked and shiny lino, were the only floor coverings he had ever known.   His openness and total appreciation of her treasured home endeared him to my mother and he was allowed into the Madden house, a fact which he proudly let be known to the rest of the gang. During the winter months, when he looked particularly ill and cold, I would sit him on our front step and feed him meat sandwiches, a luxury that I assumed he could not afford. Little did I realise that the amount of meat being consumed in their household was worthy of a butcher's shop!

My sister and I were three years older than Shendy and the prospect of Grammar School began to loom again. We became the educational guinea pigs in a 15+ transfer which would remove us from the Secondary Modern in one quick swipe to place us back amongst our 11+ successful peers. Only one pupil had gone before, a boy named Michael Gresty, who had left the Boys' Secondary Modern to earn a reputation as a formidable scholar at Crewe Grammar School. Caught up in this adventure, our uniforms were purchased and we visited the Grammar School to collect our books before the summer holidays, in order to at least have some preparation before we entered the fifth ' O' level year. We tested out our brown macs by wearing them over to the Mill and people commented favourably. Many of our peers were leaving school for work and we even knew of one girl with a baby! We felt secure and comfortable with our friends, although a little nervous of what lay ahead.

For months I had not seen Shendy; someone said that he had been ill. When he finally appeared again we were shocked by his sickly appearance. He was a deathly white and so thin that we all felt pangs of worry. Even the toughest of boys jostled to get closer to examine him in detail. Peeling down the baggy trousers, he showed us a raw red scar worthy of a battle wound. One night, after work, he had fallen over in agony after complaining of stomach pains for weeks. Realising that he was possibly dying, he was placed on the back of his brother Harry's motorbike and driven semiconscious to the Crewe Memorial Hospital. His appendix had burst and the young doctor on duty that night had never performed an operation before. Of course there was no choice and no time for alternative decisions and he saved Shendy's life, making an emergency incision within minutes of the poor boy entering the hospital. Weeks of convalescing followed before Shendy was off the danger list. During that time, he and a schoolteacher friend completed a jigsaw so large that it was placed under glass for all to see. I stared at this white faced boy and I trembled to think of his suffering. Then I noticed that I was looking at him, not down at him. He had grown to my height in that short time.

When Shendy was fourteen and a half, his Dad died quite suddenly of thrombosis. Shendy used to tell us about his Dad's illness. A clot of blood would eventually move through his body to his heart and he knew of this. At nights, when his last-born child came in from the butcher's shop, he would be waiting with food and a hot drink and the two of them would talk. Finally, his father would write a beautifully scribed letter for school to excuse his son's lateness.

He told Shendy wonderful stories of his experiences as the son of a gamekeeper of Crewe Hall Woods. He would call foxes to his side and could see in the dark! He was so in tune with nature that his power over animals was extraordinary. He understood their sicknesses and fears. The gypsies often came to him for advice.

He had fought in two world wars and married his wife at the age of sixteen. It was a true love match and they were carried to the church in a carriage pulled by two white horses. Now he was dying and there was not a moment to be lost as he endeavoured to pass down some of his wisdom to his favourite son. We all knew when Shendy's father died for it was the first and only time that we saw him silent and subdued.

The roughest of boys challenged him, throwing big arms around his thin shoulders in an effort to break through his terrible mourning. Later he confided in me, describing the last hours with his father who would die of a stroke in the early hours of the following morning. Shendy did not suspect that the long lasting illness would move so swiftly and he was heartbroken.

On the day of the funeral he spoke to his aunty in the front room of the house. She said that her only brother, Arthur, loved flowers and swiftly Shendy asked her why she had never bought him any during his lifetime! His father's only sister was extremely wealthy, owning a nursery and factories and she supplied two of the cars for the funeral. Shendy refused to travel in them and rode behind the funeral procession on his bike. As they entered Crewe Cemetery, the vicar apprehended the grief stricken boy on the old machine and ordered him from the cemetery. Did he not know that there was a funeral taking place and that people were respectably dressed!

Shendy shouted out that it was his Dad that was being buried and the vicar apologised, stunned by the incident. So it was that Shendy saw his father lowered into his grave and alongside his own poor childhood was buried.

The boy was left with his mother and he became a man overnight. The visits to the mill became less and less as he took on a full time job at a poultry packing station to support the home. For a number of years his dream had been to go to sea, following in the footsteps of his hero, his older brother, Eddie. He had saved over the years for clothes and a cycle and finally a Velocette motorbike. Now his savings opened up prospects of a place at a Navigation Training School. He proudly told us that he had been offered a place but a year later we still spotted him in Crewe and one day I asked him why he wasn't sailing around the world.

In his usual cheerful manner, which brushed aside all self indulgence, he told me that his mother had grieved so much over the death of her husband that he drew his entire savings from the bank, thirty pounds in all, and booked a week's holiday at Blackpool. He gave his mother pocket money, they ate in restaurants where they left sixpence tips for waiters and while she sat on a deckchair on the beach, Shendy hired a boat that was propelled by water wheels and challenged the murky waters, dreaming of a life at sea.

Two years later, Shendy was gone and we heard exciting stories of his travels around the world through his mother's neighbour, Mrs Green. When he jumped ship in Montreal, Canada, he reached Buffalo, New York, before being placed on board ship again. He was endeavouring to reach his one sister who had left the folds of the family to marry a GI and live in America. He did not even have her address or know her married name, but homesickness had swamped him and he was convinced he would be able to find her.

I never saw him again until I was married. My sister and I were visiting our parents when a knock came on the front door. We opened it to a tall, handsome young man with a disarming smile. It was Shendy, home from his travels and armed with evidence in the form of slides and photographs. He was twenty-one years of age and as my sister and I sat with the two boring young men who we had brought along with us, we felt thrilled to see our lively friend who told stories that shocked and delighted us.

My mother fussed around him, confident now because we were both 'spoken for', for even she could not fail to recognise his attraction. My father chuckled as Shendy showed slides of his world travels, every now and then popping a slide of nude women in between the pictures of South America, Africa and Australia. My mother never even noticed and we laughed with delight because he represented that wonderful part of our childhood, the part that could never be claimed by anyone else.

That day the door of our childhood finally closed but unknown to us, its ghosts and images would dance by our sides, affecting our lives forever.

Swans

A sultry day for a pleasure trip
and mesmerised by the unwavering cut
and the sick motor tap tapping,
you go wild, punch-drunk with bravado.
There's a whiff of diesel,
a cocktail of lethargy and indulgence,
a shot of anxiety and lust.

We approach a group of swans
snug in thick luscious grass,
preening each other like pretentious girls,
who, seeing us, totter in
and flake out behind like a white wedding.
Hall mark silver, all dressed up
each faithful pair playing gooseberry.

We feed them bread, but still they follow
rubber necking, inquisitive, thick as thieves.
chaperoning

The canal glistens
and our walnut boat trickles higgledy-piggledy
dunks against the edge of wilderness
as the swans soft peddle, seethe and make off,
and we float into unknown territory

Ryan Ó Conaill

Michael

My adventures in Scotland were still to come when I went hiking in North Wales with my friend Judith, and during a two-night stay at a youth hostel in the Llanberis Pass, I met a boy who came from Worthing in the South of England. During the evenings we spent time in the common room occupying ourselves with the limited resources such as the worn ping pong table, board games and in my case, the few well-used books in the old bookcase. I was reading some poetry by Rupert Brooke when I became aware of a tall fair-haired boy standing behind me, looking over my shoulder.

The two poems that I discovered that evening so long ago have remained meaningful to me since; Pine Trees And The Sky: Evening and The Hill. Such passionate words written by a man long dead. But it was Brooke's poem entitled The Hill that really held so much that was personal to my sixteen years, bringing tears to my eyes as I read it.

I closed the book; placing it carefully back alongside other ancients. Turning, I confronted the boy who read over my shoulder. Looking into his narrowed grey eyes I sensed both unease and curiosity. So we sat and talked into the night. He was fifteen and exploring Wales with his friend before facing a year of exams at school. His southern accent and thinking intrigued me but nothing more. As young people do, we exchanged addresses and from time to time we wrote to each other.

His father was a vicar and he too was expected to go into the ministry. 'O' levels passed to 'A' levels, which he studied at a boys' public school and I would listen with interest to the rules and traditions of his school, which differed so much from the grammar school that I attended.

Creeping into his letters were references to painting and possible art college. My twin sister was involved with a boy who also painted and so it was that he came up from Worthing and celebrated our twenty-first birthday with us.

After his visit, it was my turn to travel down to the south coast and meet his parents and sister, who was an actress in London. The picture began to widen as I spent my first Christmas away from home. This was the first time that I had broken with our family tradition and I knew that I would miss those special days spent at my grandmother's house surrounded by the many memories from my childhood, but I was curious to see how this day would be celebrated in Michael's house.

Excited and happy to see Michael, I joined in the detailed preparations with enthusiasm. On Christmas Eve the best silver was cleaned and polished; the finest glasses emerged from a previously locked cupboard; a porcelain dinner service preserved for special occasions such as this was set out on a linen cloth, an heirloom on Michael's mother's side, and a number of drinks were placed on the sideboard. The Christmas turkey packed with stuffing and various meats had already been prepared and there was a sense of order even before the important day.

The strange thing was the absence of smells, heat from a fire fuelled oven or the sounds of bubbling food. There was no shouting from Cissie as my grandmother told her off for putting lipstick on and dressing up for Christmas Eve activities and there was no feeling of excitement in the pit of my stomach, even though present giving by means of a pillow case of toys at the foot of our bed had long since gone, in fact this was just a timetable carried out with precision. In a word, it was boring and looking around at everyone I sensed that too. It was just an event to be attended to and I began to dread the big day and to wish that I was home where things were unfolding, changing, moving. I don't remember laughing at all on that Christmas Eve and I made the fatal mistake in front of the family by announcing that I didn't want to attend any church services!

Michael and I felt the same way about so much false ceremony and I supposed we rebelled, hugging and kissing in the kitchen behind the door, sneaking down to the beach after dark and exchanging stories about Christmases past. His memories were nondescript and predictable. There had never been such a thing as a 'row' in his house, for shouting was not tolerated. Everyone bubbled away within themselves, but played a pleasant social game with one another.

So I made Michael laugh as I spinned the Neville Street events, even telling him of the men Cissie used to meet and how I used to walk with her across the field at the top of Neville Street to kiss her goodbye in front of a man impatient to take her off on clandestine business. I would warm to these reminiscences and he would encourage me to talk. Once he even asked me if all girls in the North of England wore knickers as he had heard this from his school friends and it had jokingly been backed up by his teachers!

That Christmas day when everyone was at church he and I climbed the stairs to his bedroom where carefully and solemnly we undressed and lay in full daylight on his bed. There were to be so many unspoken words between us, but we made love slowly and carefully at first, for neither of us had ever been involved in any physical relationship. As we shyly twined around each other we each released a passion, creating a great longing in both of us.

I remember lying in his arms watching the room growing darker and eventually emerging and coming down the stairs soundlessly. Later we joined in the traditional mince pies and Christmas tea, looking across the afternoon tea trolley at each other but giving no secret away before his mother ran us as far as Brighton to look at the outside of his school, which his father had attended in the past.

But I looked at the boy with the strange grey eyes and knew that day that his parents' plans for him were theirs alone. The following May I travelled down again to his home, declaring myself 'in love' to my entire family, who may have been concerned but never tried to dissuade me. This time I entered the school, for although he was a weekly boarder, he was allowed visitors. That day we sat on the hallowed ground of the playing fields and he asked me to marry him. Searching in his blazer pocket he produced a single diamond ring and placed it on my finger. Looking back I smile to think of that childish and precious moment, for culturally we were so different. I came from a world of steam trains, allotments, a family who loved me but did not impose their will on me and a twin sister who had a wicked sense of humour.

His world, which I stood on the edge of, was comprised of set values, no risk taking and following in the father's footsteps. Anyone who has lived in the north of England understands those clear but invisible lines that separate us from the South. It isn't merely accent, but a deeply entrenched feeling of 'being better, posher, richer or even if you're poor you have the old guidelines to stick to', which somehow made you superior to 'those up north'.

This class distinction between North and South is blurred now but it still exists. In 1961 it was thriving, an entrenched social system that resulted in so much harm for the individual. So there we were, engaged, in love, making love and growing briefly together. Of course the religious hold fell away and he applied for and gained a place at the London School Of Film. I have vague memories of small clips of film being made in Brighton and then the big move to London where he lived for a while in a flat in Wandsworth.

Spring day – lying in his single bed and the net curtain blowing across our bodies, the landlady waiting cat-like on the stairs to pounce on us when we crept out. Another day – summer this time, when he covered my body with buttercups and daisies as we lay on the single bed, happy times before his mother's illness and death from cancer in a London hospital.

She gave him sufficient money to buy an old barge, which we moored on the Thames. The popular song 'Michael rowed the boat ashore' would ring out as we climbed from the rowing boat onto the creaking wooden timbers of the old boat, laughing at the unusual bed and on-board accommodation. We had spotted the barge one day when we were wandering by the river. Negotiations were long, finalised only by a cash deal. It was a leaky old vessel that smelt of mildew and damp but for months it gave us a meeting place until one day it simply sank!

But the north was pulling me back. Imperceptibly but powerfully it wrapped around me with its Lowry landscapes and its Ted Hughes poetry. Bit by bit I began to return to a meaningful world, reading letters from Ted to my students. I travelled by steam train up and down the country every weekend to meet with Michael, for I was teaching by now and that world was claiming me, the little diamond ring my only evidence of another life.

One day Michael didn't answer my telephone calls. He was now living in Sloane Square with a young man whose name was the same as ours. His network of friends began to include people from the film world and I knew that we were moving apart from each other.

I travelled down to Euston from Manchester one winter weekend, remained all night on the station and rang until he returned to his flat. When he came to the station I just had time to hand him the ring before boarding the north bound train. My last memory of him was turning briefly to see that he too was crying and calling me to come back. But I instinctively knew that if I remained in London, in his world Janice Madden would disappear forever.

On the lonely train journey back north to Crewe, I thought about the relationship, realising how much his mother had loved him. Before his mother died she had told me that both he and his sister were adopted, but somehow I already knew that, even back in the youth hostel when I detected his loneliness and lack of identity.

I trudged home through the familiar streets to Crewe, taking the easier route along Nantwich Road. Turning down Ernest Street I deliberately walked through the piles of snow brushed from people's doorsteps, called out to neighbours, glanced up the 'backses' to see if 'Our Dad' was anywhere to be seen and finally turned in at the gate of my house. Home at last! What had started out so hopefully was now a weight released.

Spring Opening

Bees the size of golf balls
ping over the fairway
into the flags of new flowers
to gorge on pollen
awaking lovers,
who, high with incense
and the end of innocence
are greedy for one another's sweetness.

They lie together
ready for a frenzy of loving
and douse each other with dew.

Later, the stings and bites
of swollen emotions
need a poultice to lessen the pain.

Ryan Ó Conaill

Postcard from Iona

I anxiously awaited a letter from Scotland, a promise made to me by a young man who talked of adventures which I could only dream of. At the age of eighteen, I had already declared myself a traveller. An avid reader, I was propelled through literature and autobiographies to lands far away. In reality I had never left Cheshire, apart from one ambitious hiking expedition with my friend Judith, to North Wales.

My imagination was fired by talk amongst a group of school friends who had gathered together one night to share stories and cider. I attended a co-ed Grammar School and mixed easily with the opposite sex. Strange as it seems, in the light of today's youth, we did not wish to engage in romance but rather talked of our futures, hopes and dreams.

The young man came from a local boy's Grammar School and was admired by all as one of their most talented rugby players. He laughed a great deal, was strong and confident and was not from Cheshire. He did not have our local singsong accent but rather an Americanised voice which spoke with authority knowledge beyond his years. I was curious. I drew closer to look at this stranger. He was built like an ox and was about five foot ten inches tall. His blond hair curled into the back of his neck and he was bronzed, unlike the rest of us at the close of an English winter. In fact, he resembled a young god of bygone ages. I was fascinated by his talk of America and his life abroad.

Later that evening, he sought me out and so began a fascinating conversation. He was a year older than me and he had indeed led a charmed life. His name was Peter and his father worked for the Shell Oil Company, thus the entire family had lived in exotic locations across the world for many years. He was completing his 'A' levels before entering a British university. I was tongue-tied. I had to rely on the contents of travel books, and my only expedition to Wales, for conversation.

He was a rock climber and constantly returned to Scotland, where he risked life and limb on the face of some of the highest mountains in the United Kingdom. I admired him tremendously and listened in admiration to this self-assured young god. As we talked that night in the crowded room, I joined him in his travels. I wanted similar experiences and I became fascinated with the thought that maybe I could spend time with such a lively travelling companion. He felt very safe to be with.

In today's young society, many a young woman would have thought of sexual connotations, not rock climbing, but I saw him like a painting or a superb piece of sculpture. If I had reached out and touched him it would have meant touching something in awe and admiration.

Suddenly he reached out and threw a strong, confident arm around me. As I realised that he was asking me to be his companion and to accompany him on his treks up north I was speechless and shy. He must write, I told him and I would reply. Maybe I would take up his offer. That night, as my sister and I returned home, I could think of nothing else. So began the long wait for the letter.

It arrived within a few weeks with the postmark "OBAN" on it. Hastily I found the atlas and tracked the name down to a destination far north on the west side of the Scottish coast. Beyond, scattered large and small, were many small islands and to the north lay Skye where he intended to climb the Cuillins.

Visiting the local library, for the first time I examined in detail the maps of the west coast of Scotland - Eigg, Rhum, Mull and Skye. A thousand wonderful place names conjured up for me a country of mystery and great beauty. I imagined Peter moving easily and confidently amongst the locals; self-motivated and cheerful, challenging his very being on lonely rock faces and pitching his one man tent in some quiet valley cradled deeply in the side of the mountains. How I envied him. I must go north and experience these things, to share and delight in them with a fellow traveller.

My parents were cautious. I planned to go with my friend Judith and we would camp together. Carrying bulging haversacks and with very little money, we set off by train for Oban. I could not reply to Peter by letter, as there was no forwarding address, only a post office on Skye. I sent a postcard stating the date of our arrival and our adventure began.

As the train travelled north, Judith and I pored over maps, discussed plans and grew excited as towns gave way to Yorkshire hills, then vast tracts of sheep land and finally Glasgow. The steam train sped north, carrying with it all our dreams and expectations. Looking out of the carriage windows we saw little townships isolated and remote from city life and finally mountains, several still snow-covered.

At six that evening, two weary travellers alighted at Oban station. The youth hostel lay on the far side of an enchanting town, perched on the edge of the Firth of Lorne, bathed in inky blue moonlight. Beyond, lay dark shapes resting in still water, the beginnings of the Inner Hebrides.

The following morning we set off by ferry for Skye. The sea journey carried us past islands whose secrets were darkly withheld. Married to the sea, they remained aloof and enticing. Deep below us lay green seas teaming with silver fish. Such beauty astonished me. Finally, we arrived on Skye along with other travellers, all suitably dressed for harsher climates. That night we camped near the jetty.

The following day, we headed for the Cuillins, the mountain range that lay formidable and dark. The landscape was vast, the only movement being the crashing waterfalls and wheeling birds. Far above us, climbers were roped in unison as they silently descended sheer rock faces. I wondered if Peter was one of those tiny figures. There was no word at the post office. My postcard lay in the rack, uncollected.

I wrote home asking if any letters had arrived and by return post my mother sent me another letter from Peter. He had left Skye and journeyed on across Mull to an island called Iona. Here he was helping to rebuild an ancient abbey and would I join him there? The letter gave clear instructions on how to cross by ferry from Oban to Mull. There I must take a bus and travel for a number of hours before reaching the far side of the island. Then a small ferry would carry me across the Iona Sound on to Iona itself. He also wrote of the abbey and the restoration work needed. He was involved in the building programme that would restore this ancient abbey to its original splendour.

So began a long trek to Iona with nights spent under skies filled with stars and days spent avidly discussing plans as we made our way across Mull by local bus.

The island of Mull, strong, silent and brooding, led us across its ancient pathways towards an unknown destination, a tiny island that would remain within my memory forever. Iona; Scotland's sacred isle, which had spread Christianity across the land. Its monks lighted Lindisfarne's lamp and carried Celtic learning as far as Switzerland. Kings borne to burial in its hallowed soil included Macbeth and the murdered Duncan. It was on this small island that St Columba founded Iona monastery in AD563.

Many years later, I would feel again that affinity with Iona, when I set foot on Delos, the sacred Greek Island, birthplace of Apollo and Diana, which lay at the centre of the Kikladhes in the Aegean sea. It was here where I sat amongst the ruins of temples and reflected on that other time long ago when I stood at the beginning of my life. Delos was a great comfort to me at a time of loss and sadness. Iona allowed me to rejoice with the innocence of an eighteen-year-old girl.

So we journeyed across to Iona that evening, a sea voyage of such intensity and hope. Around us lay waters, deep and calm, behind us rested Mull, the gatekeeper, and beyond us were unknown oceans. Iona, low lying, silent and anonymous welcomed us as her children and enfolded us in her misty blue cloak. We became part of her.

TENT ON IONA, JANICE CAMPING ON IONA

On that first night we pitched our tent to the south, overlooking a bay, so untouched by human hands that we could only stare, silent and lost for words. Beneath our feet lay fragile flowers and violet heathers, blossoming in the short summer. There was no sign of people, buildings or of the mysterious abbey where Peter would be.

I climbed to the top of a grassy mound and gazed in every direction. Mull was now lost in darkness. The ferryman's boat was pulled up onto an empty beach and everywhere was bathed in a turquoise light. I felt overwhelmed by such beauty, knelt down on the short grass and prayed; fervently and passionately for my safe journey. The wind blew over me, carrying my thoughts far away. The ground beneath my feet became a strength, it was father and mother to me. I knew in that moment of time that one day, years later, I would again stand on the little hill and offer my thoughts to the wind.

The following day I discovered the abbey and came across no one. Signs of reclamation lay about in the forms of large slabs of stone and evidence of building work but there were no people. I wrote my name in the visitors' book and looked through it for Peter's signature but there was nothing. The abbey itself was cold and silent; I was overawed by its strength of purpose and sensed an indifference to individuals. It has served a far greater purpose, witnessed sacrifice and dedication. I was humbled.

So began many weeks living on Iona. When our money ran out we took work on a farm. We endured a little of the hardships of the crofter. Windstorms shattered the Sound, the short stretch of ocean becoming a mountainous sea, cutting us off from Mull. I saw maggots washed from meat, oven bread supplementing plain diets and began to learn a little of the nature of people who endure island life. The windstorms would lift and Iona would once again offer itself for short periods of time to the mainland. There was a rhythm to the living and I became part of its pulse.

My search for Peter ended long ago when I discovered that within two days of reaching Iona he had returned to Cheshire to meet his family. I never made contact with my fellow traveller again and often wondered what became of him. Did he continue on his journey as I have done? Did he seek far away places and rejoice in them?

Certainly he led me forwards, walking ahead of me just out of sight in order that my journey never be completed.

Iona Abbey

How to rebuild the ruins?
It refused to reveal its secrets.
Solutions were illusive as clear days
of unending black rainstorms
narrowing in from the Cuillins
swamping the Island of the dead,
and in the ocean sharks
circled like bad omens

We anointed the foundations
with whiskey, toasting
the medieval builders
scrawled our names,
said our piece,
left a message for the Celtic Saints
buried with the bottle.

After that
God guided our hands
drew us pictures
gave us insight
He puzzled over possibilities,
gave us probabilities,
handed us solutions,
intuition to calculate
curious sizes and angles,
to raise the ancient cloisters
without the need for drawings.

Kneel and pray at this spot
remember us.
See our youthful faces in carvings
our handiwork on every set and levelled arch
find inspiration in a corbelled window.
deepen optimism, conquer doubt
make a cathedral out of your chamber
a community out of a hiding place

Ryan Ó Conaill

Chapter Three:

Going North 1961 - 1964

Two Poets

My father always refrained from interfering in our young adult lives, but I recall one occasion when he reversed a decision that I had made without even consulting me. I was launched into teaching at the age of twenty-one, idealistic, a lover of language, an innocent to the teaching profession. I had asked for a school in the centre of Manchester. Here I could show children the beauty of Lawrence's writing, walk them side by side with Shakespeare and help to create within them the love of language. Or so I imagined!

I was invited to spend a day at the school where I was to teach. Part of my responsibility was care of the library, together with a number of senior English classes. The head of the English faculty could not be traced. A bitter and weary secretary showed me to his room and left. I knocked on the door and a well-spoken voice answered. Finally, the key turned in the lock and I was confronted by a prematurely aged man of around forty years. He quickly locked us into the room and proceeded to babble on about the school and its horrendous social problems.

Most of the area had been cleared and residents moved to high-rise flats. Grimly, many families hung on to their terraced houses, refusing to surrender their stability and neighbourhood friends despite abysmal living conditions. Thrown into a dilemma, the council tried repeatedly to re-house the poor families, finally surrendering to their temporary wishes. So the school took in the remaining boys and girls until finally the entire area was zoned for compulsory demolition.

The teacher waved an exhausted hand in the air. He felt that he had lost the battle for education. Depression and total abject gloom filled the room. Why couldn't these people see the necessity of a move to a new high-rise life? Ironically time has revealed that these miserable people were correct in their intuitive thinking; life was far poorer once their little communities had broken up. They must have sensed that their happiest times were spent right here in the poverty stricken inner city and not in the future isolation of an architect's dream.

The teacher sadly shook his head. His was a nightmare world of necessity. Dusty books lay on a desk, which separated his knowledge from the battle zone of the defiant pupils. He slumped wearily onto a chair and stared at me. Why had I come here he demanded angrily. It became clear he hated my optimism. Maybe I reminded him of himself twenty years ago. I was not deterred. Where was the library? Would he please show me? Angrily he began to explain that the few remaining books had been locked away in the inner sanctum of the headmaster's office. The pupils had pushed most books down the lavatories. His fragile sanity was temporarily restored by barricading himself into his classroom during each lunch hour!

On the train journey home I set about convincing myself of the necessity of working in such a place. I would be the light at the end of the tunnel for these pupils. When I told my father of my visit, he listened carefully then left the room, appearing briefly to speak to my mother. Several hours later he returned, walking calmly into the house. I was surprised to note that he was wearing his best suit.

He sat down and told me that he had travelled to Manchester, visited the Education Department and changed my appointment to another more hopeful school. I was shocked at the time, but now I am eternally grateful for the decision made by my father all those years ago. I am still teaching and have maintained my energy and hope. A few weeks in such a school would have destroyed my idealism. My career would surely have ended there and then in that inner city school.

So I found myself at Plymouth Grove Girls' School in Longsight, Manchester. Coming, as I had, from a very pleasant rural area of Cheshire, it was still quite a shock to me. But I experienced an amazing year building up skills that enabled me to survive at the coalface of teaching. My classroom was on the second floor and had bars at the window because truanting boys threw bricks up to distract the girls, but within its four walls was a great sense of peace and discipline.

My twin sister and I rented a small flat and we lived in Manchester for a year, walking to our respective schools through streets and past parks that were the subjects of L.S. Lowry's paintings. Strangely, I can never remember feeling despondent. As my sister planted and grew sunflowers that sprouted from dustbins in the playground of her primary school, I threw myself into teaching language within a classroom where pupils rested temporarily before leaving at fifteen for factory work.

I discovered several remarkable pupils who grew to love the language of poetry. I recall a remarkable poem by a girl named Rita Gallagher. She had a paper round very early each morning, loving the small streets and silent main road. The unaccustomed silence overwhelmed her. Apart from the occasional large rat that ran along the gutters and the old newspapers that blew across the roads, there was no sound. Rita grew to love this time of day, claiming it as her own and she wrote a remarkable poem about it.

First class at Plymouth Grove Girls School 1962
(Susan Schofield second from left)

Another pupil in the same class caught my attention almost immediately. She was a small, dreamy-eyed girl named Susan Schofield who quickly revealed an amazing ability to write. Her brightness and sharp observations had attracted the attention of all the teachers and she was considered by all to have great potential. Unfortunately, this could not be realised because of financial restraints and she would later leave school prematurely for the workforce along with the other girls.

I was privileged to work with this gifted girl for several months. We taped the writings of her class, including several remarkable poems of her own, and, working alongside the BBC's Listening and Writing programme, we had the pleasure of listening to the poetry being broadcast one school morning.

Across the road inside a factory, many of the mothers of these girls also listened to the broadcast as they worked, their hearts swelling with pride.

Susan was a natural writer and artist. She reached across boundaries with ease, comfortable with centuries old poetry. At the age of thirteen she was a poet. Pale faced, her intense blue eyes fixed upon the complexity of language created in another century. She could relate to it so easily that she might have been by the writer's side.

As her teacher, I was curious. As much as I gave her to read, she absorbed critically with a sharp air of observation and often-cynical humour. She consumed knowledge with ease, also creating her own work with sparkling originality.

As a class, we became involved with a poet who at that time was beginning to make himself known to schools across England through the BBC programs. He initiated several of the writing sessions, which we pursued via the radio in our little northern English classroom. Susan developed an affinity with this poet and through the programme she wrote several letters to him. When he replied it inspired her to produce more work.

Towards the end of my year at the school, we were also in touch with L.S. Lowry, who lived near to Manchester. He wrote long letters to the pupils, ending with little drawings of matchstick men. I remember telling the pupils to keep the letters in a safe place as one day they would be of significance. I have often wondered what became of them.

During my last few weeks at Plymouth Grove School, Susan rushed up to me one day holding a letter sent from her fellow poet. She wanted to share his news with me. I read with interest that he was to attend an important interview at the BBC and to bring him luck he vowed that he would carry Susan's letter in his top pocket. I will never forget the look of pleasure and delight on her face.

Now her poet has joined the ranks of the immortal Poets Laureate. His name will be preserved for eternity alongside Wordsworth, Tennyson and Betjman.

Ted Hughes, Poet Laureate to the Queen, thank you for taking the time to reply to a very gifted pupil. That moment, standing in the schoolyard in the autumn of 1961, holding your letter, provided her with the reality of writing. It was then that your poem Thought Fox came alive and in a strange and unaccountable way, for that brief moment in time, you inspired one another with the 'spirit of the Bard'.

Skipping

JANICE AND SOUTH AFRICAN FRIEND PAUL
Newcastle Upon Tyne 1962

My enthusiasm for teaching remained undiminished and as Plymouth Girls' School was to be pulled down as part of the inevitable move towards the 'high rise living' and the surrounding area about to be bulldozed into islands of mud and derelict buildings, I began to look further afield for jobs.

My twin sister had already decided to return to the family home and teach locally, whereas I decided on Newcastle Upon Tyne as my next location. Travelling up by train that late summer of 1962 took me into a fascinating part of England, which I knew little about. My appointment was once again at a secondary school for girls, a dockside school in a poverty stricken area. Here I found a rich community of redundant miners and families existing on the dole. Most children had free meals but their enthusiasm for knowledge was supported by powerful mothers who attended all the parents' evenings, sometimes in their pinnies as they returned from their part time work.

The winters were vicious, for I had only known Cheshire snows. It was something of a shock when the first heavy snow fall prevented me from leaving my flat in Jesmond and it was eventually those Arctic winters that caused me to return to the North West. This however was not before I fell foul of the formidable headmistress, who, tight lipped and unsmiling, ruled the school with a joyless discipline that all the children accepted.

Her interpretation of leadership skills came in one short sentence,

"I know these people, and you don't."

I never quite understood her painful task of running a school brimful with such hopeful girls so I avoided her until one spring day when she summoned me to her office. It was a particularly bright and sunny morning and I felt happy with the world in general and in particular with the lessons I had planned. That morning I had made the fateful mistake of skipping across the grey tarmac playground in full view of the headmistress's office, which had been purposely chosen so that she had an eagle's view of the yard.

With growing dread I climbed the stone stairs to her room and knocked on her door. Whatever could be wrong? I knew that last week I had written 'higher purchase' on the blackboard instead of 'hire purchase', but all the girls thought that it was a clever way to explain the pitfalls of such a system of buying goods and I'd made quite sure that the monitor had erased my mistake at the end of the lesson. No, I could think of nothing wrong.

The dark, turret shaped room reminded me of an antechamber to a prison. Everything in there appeared to be grey or black. Light filtered through a small window in front of which sat a huge heavy desk, which was strangely empty of papers. The headmistress sat perched behind the desk on a high chair. Her grey hair was held back in a tight bun and the steely glasses on the end of her nose completed a picture of alarming sterility. I subconsciously tugged at my skirt, which suddenly felt too short, and tried to smile.

"Yes, do you wish to speak to me?"

"Miss Madden, Do you realise what you have done?"

"Err, no. I'm sorry, but no I can't think of anything."

The icy one rose to her feet. Although she was barely five feet tall I sensed her looming presence. She stepped from behind her desk and I noted her black thirty-denier stockings, her black laced up shoes and as my eyes travelled upwards, her belt from which hung the entire school key collection! Then I was looking into grey fish eyes made large by the much-magnified spectacles.

"Miss Madden, when you entered the school grounds this morning, you skipped across my school yard. Please explain yourself."

I felt hysterical laughter rising within myself. "Well Headmistress, I felt happy," I said lamely.

Suddenly she darted forward on the word 'happy' and shook with rage. "You have no right to show your personal feelings! This is a school where learning takes place. We must not confuse learning with feelings. You will have the girls feeling happy next and goodness knows where that will lead to!"

With that, she opened the door as a dismissal and I stepped outside and now when I reflect upon that incident, one thing comes to mind. There was not a single book in her room!

I knew that I would be looking for another teaching post at the end of the year, but during my remaining time in Newcastle Upon Tyne I must have completed a PhD in happiness, for my lessons began with jokes and they ended with jokes. I taught the girls to dance, write poetry, keep diaries and record all amusing incidents and on my last day, I skipped all the way across the playground and out of the school gate!

Skipping Song

Unravel it, you can twist, swing or skip,
this rope can whip you hang you or dance
It can bind hands, burn wrists, and trip
you up given half a chance.
This rope can pull a man, play a game,
tap a rhythm on a trap door
it can exhilarate, liberate, catch , tame
a horse, fasten it tight and rub it raw.

This rope can make you scream, start a fight,
or humiliate, maim and bruise, blur sight
then slip round a neck to tighten a noose,
or if you choose it can pull you free
stretch an arm to lift a child's kite.
and sail us away with nothing to lose.

Ryan Ó Conaill

The Christmas Carol Service

The offer of a teaching position in English and Drama drew me to the West Riding, within reach of Sheffield, where I had trained a few years earlier.

The village, stone clad and built in a valley, led on to the new secondary school, which rested in a hollow, partially protected from the cold penetrating winds off the moors. This was ancient land, marked by burial mounds where I once unearthed a stone scraper now housed in the British Museum.

The pupils came in by bus, a world away from the throbbing industrial sites of Sheffield. The majority were from farms that lay scattered across the moors beyond. Further along the road towards the church was a monastery. Occasionally the closed order of monks would emerge to sell eggs and honey to the locals, but it remained a fortress, never invaded by prying eyes, and in the autumn and winter months thick mist would blanket it from view. The church spread over a hillside, the cemetery slowly creeping like ripples in a pond around its thick stonewalls.

That year it was decided by the headmaster and staff that the church would be the most appropriate setting for the Christmas carol service and I was asked to do one of the nativity readings and produce the dramatic image of the entire nativity. This was a formidable task for a twenty-three year old teacher, and I vowed that it would be an occasion that we would always remember. It certainly proved to be just that but I could never have imagined why at the time. There are a number of old pupils, some of them still possibly still living in the area, who will never forget our presentation. Neither will I!

And so the months of preparation began. I organised a group of 15 excellent poetry readers from the senior end of the school. They would produce the choral verse, which would flow through the service, providing the rich oral background for the nativity players.

I could visualise it all; the ancient church, the hushed congregation, the slowly moving figures of Mary and Joseph as they entered the church, moving down the aisle to the sounds of the choral speakers and finally reaching their positions near to the altar to begin the formation of the tableaux. Then would come the shepherds and the wise men.

> *'A cold coming we had of it,*
> *Just the worst time of the year*
> *For a journey...'*

In that bleak mid-winter, high up on the moors, a little church would resound with the well rehearsed voices of my dedicated choir of choral speakers who would immortalise this Christmas service like no other! Rehearsals commenced immediately once the summer holidays ended in August. The poetry was carefully chosen, eleven readings in all, and the pupils set about learning their lines. The nativity players were chosen from many would be candidates, as the entire school became enthused by my vision of perfection!

Then began the long walks from the school to the church, passing the monastery on our right and beyond lay the moors, which nearly always faded into the mist. Those autumnal days offered us pleasant memories of fading afternoon sun, long shadows traced the outlines of the mysterious burial mounds and untouched hollows of the moors; the last of the butterflies, fragile and windswept, would alight at our feet as we walked along chanting our lines. Finally we would approach the ancient church, push open the heavy oak door and reverently step inside onto holy ground.

We soaked in the atmosphere of that snowy Christmas night long before the evenings were cut off by darkness and thick snow, which marked a halt to our premature rehearsals. We knew by October that the entire cast would hide in the vestry at the back of the church, standing silently amongst the cassocks, choir boy robes and the many silver chalices, christening mugs and confessional goblets that lined the shelves above our heads.

Here they would wait, self disciplined and contained until the little church filled with the local community. As the words of the hymn rang out,

> *Angels from the realms of glory,*
> *Now proclaim Messiah's birth,*

they would slowly walk down the aisle and form their choral group. I felt so confident that I would not even stay with them. My band of actors and speakers would appear independent of me, and I would take my place in a front pew.

Before the final sermon, they would walk down the side aisle and shelter once again in the vestry until the church emptied. The nativity players would also join them and for the remaining thirty minutes they would quietly wait in the vestry and slip out when the church had emptied. I had planned it to perfection and at the end of the night knew I would be covered in glory!

The night arrived in an excited rush of last minute preparation and final practicing of readings. It was perfected, a perfect tableaux of the Christmas story.

A light scattering of snow greeted us as we climbed aboard the bus that would take us in advance of the congregation along the two frosty miles to the church. A huge white moon lit up the gravestones and the church. Bells rang across the moors and the final perfect scene was set.

It is the calm and silent night!
A thousand bells ring out, and throw
Their joyous peals abroad.

The words of that old hymn announced the start of our Christmas service.

Nothing could go wrong - and nothing did! The pupils were exemplary, their rendering of the poetry echoing through the church, the Biblical figures bringing tears to parents' eyes as their children enacted the age-old nativity scene. I filled with pride. All the hard work over the last few months had paid off. The vicar slightly inclined his head in recognition of our efforts as he climbed the steps to the pulpit for his sermon. I glanced around to see the smiling faces of the parents, knowing that we had achieved success as a result of meticulous planning.

O come, all ye faithful,
Joyful and triumphant,

The carol echoed around the church in a finale of a never to be forgotten occasion and then I was brushing past the winter coats and 'thank yous' to the vestry.

I brushed aside the red velvet curtain to be confronted by a wall of silence!

I smiled. "Well done, well done!" I thanked them but no one moved.

Then a little first year girl giggled nervously, which prompted Philip, the spokesperson of the group, to step forward. "We have something to tell you Miss."

He was red faced and embarrassed as he pointed at all the chalices, bowls, christening cups – every receptacle in the vestry. I looked down, for they were no longer on the shelves but placed strategically around the room. "We daren't come out, we were desperate," he said apologetically.

Every container was filled to the brim with pee!

Horror struck me! Then we started to laugh, uncontrollably, hysterically, our voices muffled by the carol singing. All the pent up emotions, and the concerns were swept away in great waves of laughter! I was catapulted into their very human dilemma. We needed to act quickly though! Snatching down the robes, we wrapped them around the receptacles, Philip hiding the largest of the chalices beneath his long black coat. Then unsmiling and ceremoniously we marched out in a single line to mingle with the congregation as they shuffled towards the door.

Led by Philip, they emptied the less than holy water over the gravestones, which bordered the path. Sneaking back into the church, we carefully placed everything back and made a pact never to reveal this incident to anybody. For as long as I remained in that school I sensed a deep camaraderie between the pupils and me. If anyone ever asked me if they could go to the toilet during one of my lessons, conspiratorial smiles would identify the Christmas players.

I wonder where my band of actors is now and if they relate their tale of the special Christmas nativity of 1964 to their children - and maybe their grandchildren?

Chapter Four:

End of Spring 1964 - 1970

Nomad

His lips were a dry valley
His eyes an empty well
His mind playing distant music
My drought years an empty shell.
I have hidden him in a bottom drawer
and placed a new one in his frame
and burnt the images he tore
after he ruined us and took no blame

My bridge crosses an empty line
My mind meanders a lonely track
I have painted companions on my path
intoxicated conversations with wine
and over my shoulder thrown my finger ring
and discovered a taste for wandering.

Ryan Ó Conaill

The Shooting of the Cuckoo

My marriage was to a pleasant young man with whom I was never in love. My passion and lust for life went so far beyond my human relationships, that I alone owned it and found no one to share my drumbeat with.

If I lay in a field of wild flowers or dropped rose petals on my head, I was alone. I told no one of the big silver moon, the empty, sea-washed beaches or pounding of my heart when my spirit became as one with nature.

And so I married the pleasant young man who played the guitar and sang to me. I hoped that maybe together we would find this elusive thing, this emotion, which would move the earth beneath us and claim us as its own. The young man did have a passion and if I had been older and travelled further along my own road of enlightenment, I would have told him to open wide his arms and embrace the spirit of music.

A transformation took place in him when he played. He sang of the ultimate feelings within his soul, and then he found his paradise. But he was unable to communicate and share his sadness and fears and I, in return, locked up my heart and knew within months of living together that he would never be at one with me. How sad; two young people who were together as two old people, passion spent before it had ever begun. Yet our marriage lasted in essence for six years, as I was resolute and determined to wait for the all-consuming light that I felt convinced would come.

I waited, sitting on the dark stairs of our flat for the key to turn in the lock when he returned from band jobs. I waited as I paced the winter beaches of North Wales or walked by rushing streams; I waited, silent and still in bed, imagining passion spent. One day I discovered that I was pregnant. I was puzzled for I could not recall any great passion that could have resulted in its creation. To this day, I cannot recall even the smallest fragment of memory relating to the beginning of my child.

I desperately wanted a mate, a soulmate with whom I could talk, walk, and share my feelings with. Now I lay on barren ground, isolated and lonely. And pregnant.

My daughter was born following birth complications, which I'm convinced were a direct result of this isolation. She was exquisite, a rosebud, reassuring my soul that indeed the Phoenix does rise from the ashes. I staunchly maintained a belief that the young man did indeed have a soul. Surely, through his songs and playing he revealed so much that he was unable to share with me. So together we stayed, each one never daring to tell the other that the void between us was for eternity.

We chose to buy a house in the countryside, deep in the heart of Cheshire, where the spring flew into our bedroom window in overpowering scents of bluebells and wild roses. Where the earth was rich and black and where, in the deep night, the nightingale sang.

Spring was upon us. Nothing could now prevent its march across the countryside. The early morning frosts gave way to the pale sunshine. First came the hedge celandines, then the cowslips, primroses and sappy bluebells. Finally, the hawthorn hedges swelled with blossoms and the Cheshire fields grew bright with buttercups.

And one day in May, the cuckoo sang in our garden. From the top of an ancient apple tree, he sang his repetitive call across the ancient countryside and back came the distant echo of his loved one. I recall the moment so clearly. I was standing on the dark earth, drinking in the cool evening air and welcoming the dusk. Swallows dipped and danced before me, as myriads of small flies, newly hatched, rose above the ground.

And the cuckoo sang.

I walked into the house, overawed by the inevitability and enormity of nature. There was the sound of a gun. The air rushed past me. My heart turned to lead. The young man came in, triumphant, proclaiming his victory. He had shot the cuckoo. He knew because he had seen it fall like a stone from the tree.

Young man, I forgave your indifference, I forgave your lack of passion, I forgave your lack of understanding, but today I relive again the murder of spring. That is how my marriage ended.

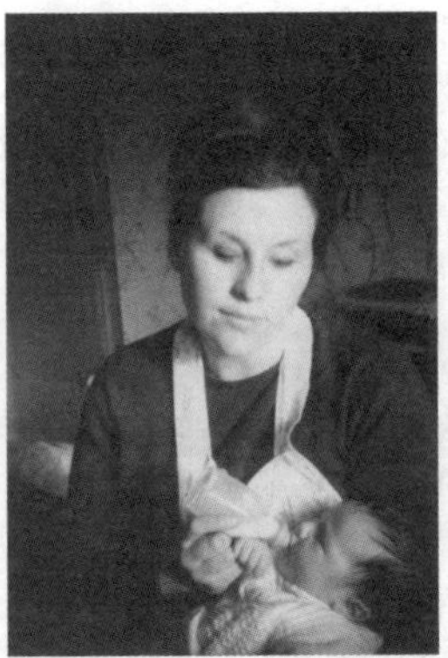

Jan and Becca, 1966.

The time of the shooting
of the cuckoo, 1967

Beginnings

Nudge the catch on the window.
Open it,
see how far your eyes follows
 the river to the sea

You see your reflection in the glasshouse.
a woman learning how to smile
hear herself laugh
take a deep breath of self esteem.
drink a tumbler full of freedom

Just take a suitcase full of hope
throw away the locks, the name tags
go to where he cannot hurt you.

What a wonderful thing is a new beginning,
It is sweeter than this misery
where you are a linnet in a soundproof cage.

Ryan Ó Conaill

The Eel

My teaching career resumed yet again in Cheshire.

The headmistress of the school had held the position for many years and her leadership skills did not include sharing and decision making with her staff. She was also obsessed by the slightest hint of sexual matters, to the great amusement of the younger members of staff who used to relate the most amazing stories regarding her insinuations. She constantly warned any member of the female staff of the dangers of starting a family as it would interfere with the running of her all girls' school and would not tolerate a male presence for very long. Even the school window cleaner was suspect and young teachers were often made extremely nervous by her sudden appearances in their classrooms and her abrupt departures.

My turn came around one day when I was teaching Geography to a fifth year class. We had reached the point in the lesson where we were looking at the continents and in particular, Africa. I had just sketched the outline of that continent on the blackboard when the door swung open and in walked the headmistress. Without a word of explanation she marched to the back of the class where she stood arms folded, waiting for me to continue.

We were all very nervous, but the lesson continued uneventfully until dismissal at the end of the day. The headmistress and I were left alone in the classroom. I began to tidy up when she cleared her throat and beckoned me to the back of the room.

"You really must consider what it is that you put up on a blackboard for all to see!" she hissed at me.

I laughed, thinking she'd gone completely mad. "I realise that my map drawing isn't very good Headmistress, but you can see that it is the outline of Africa!"

"I have never seen such a suggestive drawing!" she proclaimed. "And it must be erased at once!" And with that she thundered down to the front of the room and seizing the duster, swiped Africa off the board!

Dramatically, she swept out of the room leaving me feeling extremely puzzled. I climbed the stairs to the staff room to discuss this bizarre incident with my colleagues. The art teacher suddenly burst out laughing.

"Think about it Janice. Think about the outline of Africa. You are very guilty of a Freudian slip."

The entire incident was repeated many times and from time to time

'Africa' appeared on blackboards throughout the school, much to the horror of the headmistress who checked every board before she went home!

School became a haven for me because of the breakdown of my marriage and I was thankful for the work which kept me so busy. One day I was returning home when the screech of brakes stopped me in my tracks. A cheerful voice rand out from the sports car, "Hello, is that really you?"

I looked up from my daydreaming to see someone that I hadn't met since he'd visited my parents' home during a break from the merchant navy. Robert was my childhood friend from long ago and I couldn't have been happier to see him at this miserable point in my life. So began a number of meetings when we excitedly exchanged stories from the past, for he was also caught up in an unhappy marriage and although he was careful not to divulge too much of his personal life, I knew that the past between us had made a powerful bond.

Laughter and a deep sense of friendship gave back to me a happiness that I hadn't felt since my work in the West Riding. Together we searched out some of the old haunts of our childhood and walked across the fields towards the Mill where we had played as children.

As we talked, all these unspoken memories lay between us, erasing the loneliness and pain that comes with broken relationships.

Our meetings grew more frequent and our friendship developed, based on the many experiences we had shared as children and our need for happiness that resulted from a sharing of the many things we had in common. We spent long summer hours in the Cheshire countryside seeking yet again those pleasures that has sustained our friendship.

It was a happy time despite our many personal problems. I met Robert's many brothers and sisters and we spent time with them. As we had no permanent home Robert began to look around for somewhere to live. We had both given up our respective homes to our partners and were left with very little for ourselves. None of this seemed to matter, as we tentatively grew more hopeful of a future life together.

One of the most meaningful things that happened to us centred on a fish! It all came about in the following way.

The Pioneers' Angling Club in Crewe, Cheshire, is situated down a small side street surrounded by Northern English terraced houses. Although women frequent this fishing club it stays very much as it was intended, for men who call in for a pint of beer and a meeting place for friends.

When Crewe was a fully functioning working class town, 'The Pioneers' would be packed, the busiest times being between nine and ten thirty pm. Slowly it had to compromise, along with others and allow bingo and 'one arm bandits', but it is still run strictly on club lines; it has a visitor's book and a doorman. The older closely-knit workingmen of Crewe organise it and only members can sign in unless they enter as guests.

Inside it seems to be one of two things, either practically empty, with well worn comfortable seats grouped around individual tables waiting for their occupants and a relaxed bar staff, wiping clean the bar once too often; or thunderously full, crammed to bursting, each local taking up his favourite corner and surrounded by well-worn friends. The noise was deafening, you could cut the yellow smoke with a knife and if you were unfortunate enough to have to use the pay phone you had to shout and have an audience. At these times, you were welcomed in as a stranger, accepted only because of your silent passport - knowing someone who frequented the club.

I first visited the Pioneers Club with Robert. It was a haven for us at the end of a long day driving around or a point of contact following several hours of coarse fishing. Robert's older brother frequented the club and we would call in to exchange fishing and family news.

I was happy to sit down in the smoky crowded lounge room and listen shyly to some of the old stories. Old men who had been members of the club for years would stand up when we joined them, in deference to the fact that I was a woman. We were seen as a young couple, as legitimately together as an old married couple.

They knew 'Our Frank', the older and much respected brother of Robert, who made a daily practice of walking from his home every evening for a few whiskeys and a relaxing chat before returning home to his caring and sensitive wife.

Our relationship slowly evolved in the Pioneers and across the fields of Cheshire, feeding on those childhood memories that both of us treasured so much.

The association with the railways was strong and as Robert worked on the railway as a platelayer maintaining the rail tracks, he became part of the storytellers. He was also a very keen fisherman and on quiet afternoons he would take me into the club to show me the giant fish, preserved forever in their glass cases.

For a long time, I hadn't noticed these other occupants of the club. Placed high on the walls and in the yellowed subdued lighting they were hardly noticeable to me until pointed out. Each giant specimen represented a prize catch from river, lake or silent pool. Mounted against an artificial background of gravel and weeds, they would stare out from behind their glass prisons with glazed eyes, their silver bodies injected with preservatives, mummified trophies of death. Beneath each fish was placed a small bronze plaque which boasted the length, weight and name of the fish and the man who had caught it. Not for these fish, the natural death in the cool dark waters, or even the violent end by a predator. No – they looked down on the oldest member in the club and would with certainty outlast him.

In the dark hallway at the entrance to the Pioneers, and high up above the doors, sat a giant pike, his snapping jaws grinning in death. Stretching to a massive length it was hard to believe that such a fiendish thing could occupy a small pond for over twenty years and watch from the clouded waters as children scooped out jars of tadpoles or clambered in the bull rushes after flowers or butterflies. Capable of taking baby ducks from the surface in one giant mouthful, he was a dusty nightmare to me.

I grew into the habit of checking out each fish, waiting to see slow disintegration but the preservers in death had done their job well and these gruesome trophies continued to stare out from their glass coffins at every visit.

Then it would be out into the sunshine again with renewed plans for fishing. I accidentally discovered the essence of the Pioneers Club when we called in there one Sunday night as fishermen brought in their catches for weighing in. Such details as location, bait, and time of death were recorded accurately and weighing took place in front of solemn witnesses. Catches had to be in there by Sunday night unless you booked your day off in the week.

At this time I discovered Robert's burning ambition. He wanted to catch a prize fresh water eel! For days and days he talked about it until I too was affected by his enthusiasm. At nights when he checked the railway tracks, swinging his Tilley lamp to warn of on-coming express trains, he would be thinking of fishing line and bait, later announcing plans for the fishing trip.

We would kiss and laugh together as we stumbled across fields high in buttercups, mayflowers and long seeded grass and we would lie in bluebell woods, listening to the sound of the cuckoo and the noise of tiny insects. We would be on an expedition hunting down an overgrown pool or pond that had been casually recalled in the Pioneers or fished by Robert when he was a boy.

The summer of 1971 is captured in my mind as clearly preserved as the fish in their glass cases. I can recall the tiniest details, the shadows crossing the ploughed fields, the spinney or copses we wandered through, the delight at discovering a pond, the casting of the line onto the pollen covered surface, the roughly cut sandwiches washed down with flasks of over sweetened tea and lying deeply in corn fields and staring up at the fast moving clouds.

Chiflick Slope, Cheshire in June

In desperation, we would plan the fate of this imaginary eel. Sometimes we would even laugh over what my 'shape of Africa' obsessed Headmistress might make of our obsession with an eel! Over and over again we would relive again and again the moment when we would carry him into the Pioneers to be weighed by officialdom. He would break the Cheshire record and we would take pride of place in the local newspaper, and collect our money prize. One day in late July Robert announced the details of the fishing trip when we would catch the eel.

He had been given a permit from Bolesworth Castle to cross a Lord's land and fish in the grounds of the castle itself.

The pool lay deeply hidden in thick woodland and involved crossing several fields, which took us far from the Cheshire country lane where we had parked our vehicle.

As we approached the deeply shaded pool we fell silent. Tramping through the long grass we pushed a patch into the thick bushes and neglected remains of a garden. Huge rhododendrons stood sentinel above the dark water, and dragonflies, startled by our presence, tilted and swept above our heads, their miniature stained glass wings colouring the thick foliage. We stood at one end of a dark pool edged by cupped leaves of giant water lilies. Old worn steps led down to the water's edge on the far side but there were no signs of trampled banks or the occasional snip of fishing line.

Involuntarily I reached for Robert's hand. This was no ordinary place. I thought about the twisted stems of the lilies beneath the black water, the steep muddy banks that fell away abruptly and the cloak of thick foliage and hundred year old trees that protected it. How easy it would be to slip in and lie forever trapped in those green arms.

Robert laughed, sensing my fear. Pointing to a high bank at the western narrow end of the pool he declared it a suitable fishing spot and announced that here we would catch the prize-winning eel. We established ourselves, unpacking fishing gear, flasks, sandwiches and a green fishing box-containing row upon row of coloured floats, lead weights and silver hooks of all sizes. We did this in complete silence, Robert expertly threading the line onto the small rod that he would use. The fishing line had a four pound breaking strain. The landing net was dug into the shelving bank, in readiness.

So we sat together, two friends from childhood, two lovers in our young adults lives, side by side on the grassy bank, both lost in our own thoughts. I learnt that day that to be part of nature was to remain very quiet and still so that even the wind blowing across the pool pushing ripples before it was a disturbance. Wood pigeons cooed softly, as I lay back in the small grasses, squinting up at the leaves above me. Robert nudged me and turning on one elbow I watched three baby rabbits venture down the old brick steps.

Robert leaned back into the grass. In a low voice he began to tell me about the life of eels. They can live a long time out of water and their bodies are long and cylindrical, and only laterally flattened towards the tail. These fish have no ventral fins, and the dorsal, tail and anal fins are joined. Their gill slits are small and the scales, set in a very slimy skin, are minute.

We were fishing for the common eel that migrates into fresh water. It is a very tough creature and can withstand more pollution and difficult living conditions than any other British fish.

The eel we wanted to catch would have been bred in the Sargasso Sea between Bermuda and the Leeward Islands. Its parents would have died after giving it life and the eggs and larvae would have floated on the strong surface currents, particularly the North Atlantic Drift which slowly crosses to Europe. Our young eel would have been shaped like a laurel leaf and about 5mm in length.

After three years and by the time it reached Europe, it would have been three inches in length and be known as an elver. It would have metamorphosed into a snake like shape, and then it would have moved inshore and become pigmented. Seeking out a pool, it would have remained there until sexually mature, which could take up to twenty years. The mature female eel would be approximately twenty-four inches in length and the male sixteen inches in length. During this sexual change they would become silvery and once again migrate to the sea, returning to their place of birth where they would mate then die. Robert was hoping to capture a mature eel; The Cheshire record was set under five pounds.

My own life was one of migration and return, mingled with sexual needs and procreation. Strangely and ironically I had something in common with the eel! I said nothing of this to Robert as he bent over the tackle box, immersed in his quest, totally absorbed and understanding of the nature around him.

I thought about our eel somewhere down there in those cool still waters, and I felt shame rising in me. Did we have the right to send little silver hooks, deadly miniature spears, down into the waters, spiked into a wriggling earthworm? Why were we trying to cease a life journey?

The early morning disappeared, misted lifted and the sun parted the thick leaves of the oak and looked down on us, sitting patiently waiting for the float to be dragged under. Shadows danced across the pool but we must not move for even the slightest shudder would send warning to the big fish below.
Sandwiches were eaten, but little was said. I wondered what Robert was thinking? Did he really want to trap the eel? Shadows lengthened as evening approached and the water grew inky black. The large white water lilies began to lift the waxen petals for sleep and nothing moved. I felt relieved. We could go home empty handed.

I felt Robert's body tighten and involuntarily I looked down at the line. The float began to drift slowly, so slowly towards the large water lily pads. Was the wind blowing it? Robert slowly reached for the rod, never taking his eyes from the water. Magically, the float was gently pushing its way along the surface. Then it dipped suddenly into the blackness! In an instantaneous reflex action Robert lifted the rod and struck. The line went taut and the reel began to scream.

Jumping to his feet Robert began to play the fish expertly as it turned this way and that, churning the water into mud. Silence was shattered. I ran about the bank helplessly, not knowing what to do. The rod bent almost double but nothing emerged from the water except for giant black bubbles.

For twenty minutes Robert fought the fish that refused to show itself. Suddenly we caught a glimpse of a smooth eel head and tiny bright eyes, and then it was gone again. Pushing me out of the way, Robert tried to net it, holding the rod in his right hand, but it surged away. After several attempts of bringing the eel close to the edge, Robert put the net well behind the huge fish and then lowered the rod and let him go. The fish, feeling the slack line, backed away very quickly, shooting into the net. Robert lifted it out quickly, well up on to the bank and we both stared down at a massive eel.

We looked at one another, and thought about letting the big fish go. It had fought so bravely, it deserved to slide back into those safe waters. Robert leaned over to remove the hook then stepped back sadly. It had swallowed the hook and we both knew that this would lead to a prolonged and painful death. We kept the big eel alive, carrying it back home in a wet sack and carefully placing it in the bath at my father's house.

It weighed five pounds, eight ounces, but sadly its life ended there in Crewe, in a sterile and foreign environment. We weighed it in at the Pioneers at five pounds three ounces and it was proclaimed the biggest eel caught in Cheshire to that date. We preserved the big fish by placing it in a freezer, but we made the decision to have it mounted by a taxidermist in Yorkshire. So once more we set out on a very different type of fishing expedition, leaving the eel with the expert.

Months later we returned and collected the prize specimen. I could no longer call it the eel as I peered into the oblong glass case to see it staring out at me with those sharp, little eyes, its long liquid body tapering away into rather solid looking weed. Now it was just 'the specimen'. We had to confess though that the preservation was excellent and the eel travelled with us to our future lives in North Wales and Cornwall. Robert even used to talk to it as after a pint too many as he tottered upstairs to bed, pausing on the landing to look at it.

Finally he made the decision to give it to the Pioneers Club where it rests to this day, mounted on the wall in the lounge for everyone to see.

Fishing match

No oaths or threats
just silent combat,
the strategic shifting of seats,
and drawing of secret bait
the loading of heavy weights
a flick of wrists
with practice swings
to tilt the battle

It was a duel,
but sitting there
in cobwebs of line
a stranger wouldn't notice
this was anything more
than dangling a stick
with old string

Only his occasional
glare reminded us
there was nine pounds
at stake.

His maggoty stare
rod meeting rod
in a watery joust
touché zip of reels
as I cast away to oust
him as the Olympic God
of Haslington Pool.

He floated a hook amongst the reeds
squirmed, caught my smile,
mistook his aim and snagged against
a willow.

The stampede of feet,
his face red as raw meat
cursing swearing of oaths
as he lunged his hand
to release the fastening,
and in doing so
stumbled from dry land
into the keep net.

Going for the kill
I broke his will
and hauled in half a dozen perch
and listened to the
sniggers of happy fishermen
their eyes focused on troubled waters
in search of a bite.

Ryan Ó Conaill

Chapter Five:

Country Living 1970 - 1975

Cheshire Lane 1974

Mr Coleman

The autumn leaves lay scattered across its untidy pathway. A winter and spring had come and gone but the cottage lay silent and uninhabited. Dry leaves had escaped the disintegration reaped by winter gales, heaping together within the small paved yard, to escape cremation. Now the spring breeze pulled them easily onto the path where they willingly danced, moving like small brown mice and I walked amongst them as I made my way to the front door. It was to be our first home and I felt great relief and affection for this cottage, isolated in the Cheshire countryside.

The large key turned in the heavy oak door, which swung inwards, revealing a dinghy hallway. I was aware of the farmer apologising for the state of the place. Didn't he understand that we had nowhere to live and that we were penniless? I noted with appreciation the tiny living room and small windows, which looked out upon a lord's land, farmed for generations by his tenant farmer.

My little girls squealed with delight as they discovered the stairs and within minutes they were climbing to discover bedrooms and, beyond, the windows, which held views of the ancient castle. It was indeed a delightful cottage and we speedily made it our home. Soot was removed from the fireplace by the bucket-load and a log fire was soon burning. Within days we had found second-hand furniture and kind family members gave us bedding. By two weeks we made that little cottage into a home.

My eldest daughter began to organise the small patch of front garden. Together with her little sister, she dug the soil between the fence that separated the two halves of the cottage. The farmer had mentioned that the other half of the house was occupied by a retired farm labourer who had earned the reputation of having 'shovelled more pig-shit than any other man in Cheshire'. I gave little thought to any neighbour at all, as the place appeared to be deserted apart from the neatly clipped hedge and tidy front garden. From time to time I heard small sounds through the walls but felt no curiosity; I was far too anxious to make a home for my family, following enormous upheavals, both emotional and physical.

Almost imperceptibly, the hawthorn hedges misted into green and the giant elms shook free from their winter coats. Quite suddenly, the field opposite Dene Bank Cottage was busy with grazing cows, released from their winter shippons. Breathing steam from their nostrils, they were soon obsessed with the abundance of spring grass. In the night, they made strange unearthly noises, which I soon grew used to and even found comforting after a while.

On Sundays, our country lane became quite busy with cars carrying curious people who climbed about the ancient castle and pondered on the treasure, which is said to have been thrown deep into the well centuries ago. We fell into the rhythm of country life. It was an idyllic existence, far removed from the concrete living of the town and we felt blessed for such a home.

One day, my two girls ran into the kitchen, laughing with delight and clutching large bars of Cadbury's chocolate. Their faces gave evidence of a further bar having been consumed. Anxiously, I asked them how they had received the chocolate, thinking that a hiker passing up the lane had maybe handed it to them. In actual fact, earlier on that day, I remembered having heard them chattering away in the enclosed front garden, but paid little attention as they had imaginary friends who even had places set at the kitchen table at dinner times.

My eldest girl gave a wise smile and announced that the nice old man, our neighbour, had given them the treat, and indeed had been feeding them chocolate for several weeks, but until now they had taken their rare treasure and eaten it in the hen house at the bottom of the garden. Would I like to meet Mr

Coleman, our neighbour? Little sticky hands tugged me out into the yard and round to the front of the house and I was surprised to see an old man standing by the wooden fence.

Immediately, a pang of fear and apprehension filled me but the little girls shot forward and held his knarled hand through the fence, a rough red hand that had worked the land for over sixty-five years. Our neighbour introduced himself, quite formally extending his right hand over the fence, but not before using it in one quick swipe to wipe away what appeared to be a continually running nose. The girls were delighted that I had at last made his acquaintance and they were not in the least concerned about his surly manner and filthy clothes. An incredible smell of decay and sour milk drifted across the fence. He gave an unpleasant little chuckle and shuffled away along his path and around to his back yard. The girls sighed with contentment. He was their benefactor, their beloved friend. I was later to discover a number of shiny half crowns stowed away in their piggy banks. We were extremely poor; pocket money was out of the question and chocolate unheard of, so little treats from Mr Coleman were quite heroic to my girls.

Quickly, I hurried the girls inside, fighting down the rising fear within me. No, they had never visited his cottage. No, he had never picked them up; he had only held their tiny hands through the fence. Yes, they had taken bowls of my apple pie and custard and fed him through the fence like a baby. The girls proudly informed me that they had even given him a whole toilet roll once for his nose, but he had scuttled inside with it and the dreaded nose remained in a perpetual state of motion.

During the summer months we saw little of our strange neighbour. Weeks would pass by without a sound through the adjoining wall. Haymaking enveloped us all. Straw houses were built and home cooked food was carried out to the girls who quickly placed it in their straw kitchen. Fears and worries vanished with the summer months. Our Clumber spaniel, Tiggy, accompanied the girls on all their exploits. He became their Sir Lancelot, challenging anyone who approached them. I forgot about the neighbour, which wasn't difficult when we never saw him. We were taken up with our immediate surroundings and those early autumn days offered us all its wild and cultivated fruits. Rebecca took the largest potato ever to be seen to the harvest festival, our ferrets caught rabbits, we had fresh eggs and chicken and even our own fox and badger, the two nightly visitors to our rubbish dump. I became pregnant and preoccupied much to the girls' delight, for this gave them their freedom, which extended through the long evenings and weekends as they both now attended a little country school. I was left to my own devices. I cooked too many apple pies and began to stare a little too often across the misty Cheshire fields. I felt lonely and incapacitated.

One day I decided that I would visit our neighbour; a guilty decision as I hadn't seen him since the spring day we formally met. Plucking up courage, I took one of my redundant pies and walked along the lane and through his gate. I approached the front door and knocked but everywhere was silent. The day was grey and cold and I felt a little scared - but resolute all the same.

I strode purposefully round to the back yard, noting with approval the tidiness of the place. I knocked loudly on his back door but still there was no reply. I glanced down and noted the large hole at the bottom of the door. So that was how his cat entered and left the house.

A muttering and shuffling was followed by the door opening to reveal our neighbour, dressed in the same clothes. He did not seem surprised to see me and taking the initiative, I smiled brightly and holding the apple pie before me I stepped inside his kitchen. As I followed him into the living room, I was aware once again of the sickening smell of sour milk and old clothes. I grew determined. I would help this poor old man in every way possible.

The sparseness of his home shocked me. Mrs Coleman's influence had died with her and I could not see any evidence of a feminine hand about the place. In the grate burned a small coal fire, newspapers neatly covered the table, and the curtainless windows let in the wintry light, aided by a naked bulb, which hung from its yellowed cord. A large sideboard graced the side of one wall and heaped on it were numerous copies of the Readers Digest.

Mr Coleman motioned me to sit down and I did so, staring into a face so ancient and hard that I quailed. He had the most penetrating blue eyes and his skin was so brown and leathery that I felt an urge to reach out and touch the furrows that ran across his cheeks. He resembled the ploughed earth; he had become part of the land to which he had given his entire life.

Now he faced the fate of all Lord Tollmache's farm labourers, he was allowed to live rent free in the cottage that had once shook with the laughter and noise of his children. For there had been a family and a wife he informed me in one surly sentence that dismissed them entirely.

As we drank tea in chipped and stained cups, using condensed milk, Mr Coleman began to talk. He told me of bitter incidents involving his status on the land. One day his beloved dog had run out of the gate to meet its death under the wheels of Lord Tollmache's Rolls Royce. Mr Coleman laughed bitterly at the outcome. In a rare moment of compassion, the lord had given him one of his own puppies, which in Mr. Coleman's opinion, was useless. When the puppy disobeyed him for the first time, the old man killed it by hitting it on the head.

I shuddered. Surely he had something to comfort him, apart from such hateful memories. I asked about the cat and he chuckled, gleeful of the memory. Last winter, when the snow came down so densely that we were snowed in to our cottages for four days, Mr. Coleman sat huddled by the fire. He kept his electricity off in the evenings and dozed by his dying fire. Suddenly he was awakened by a scuttling noise and felt something warm brush against his leg. Reaching down and peering in the light from the embers he thought he saw a cat, which pressed against him for warmth.

Uncharacteristically, he fetched the cat a saucer of milk and he and his winter companion slept by the fire until the early hours. When he finally stumbled to bed, it vanished. This act of friendship was repeated during the worst of these winter nights until one evening he put on his electric light and found that his hearth companion had been a large rat. Raising the poker in disgust, he beat the big rat into a pulp. Mr Coleman stopped his storytelling to slurp down his tea in triumph. He stared at me, not wanting or needing my approval or disapproval.

I made several visits to his bleak home, hoping to find just a chink in his armour, but I was unsuccessful. Once a week he walked from the house and down to the post office to collect his pension. The walk took him most of the morning, but I never saw him leave or return. I wondered why I was even bothering to visit him as he did not appear to need anyone or anything. One day he gave my eldest daughter a beautiful book by David Attenborough, which she has to this day. Inscribed inside the front cover of the book was written, in painstakingly accurate handwriting, 'from your friend, Mr Coleman'. The book had been acquired by mail order through the Readers Digest and was much loved by the old man.

One day I was quite shocked when Mr. Coleman motioned me to look into the top drawer of his sideboard. Reaching into the deep drawers he pulled out a vast amount of paper notes. There must have been thousands of pounds. He pressed endless amounts of these notes into my hands and told me to take them. I refused to do so and feeling quite horrified, I quickly stuffed the money back into the drawers.

However, this action prompted the first and only shopping trip with Mr Coleman. I made a careful plan. I would drive him to the local supermarket and under the pretence of buying a wider variety of food, we could purchase soap powder and beautifully scented soap.

I had a vision of Mr Coleman gleaming and clean. The dreadful smells would be vanquished forever. His underwear would be snow white, his bedding freshly laundered. The girls laughed with delight at the thought of their dear friend being subjected to a little of the treatment they had to endure on a regular basis. And so the deed was done and no amount of persuasion from other family members would deter me. I was set on a course from which I would not deviate.

The shopping expedition was successful and as we filled the trolley with bleach, soap powder, Camay soap and numerous other alternative detergents, I brainwashed Mr Coleman into the necessity of a hot bath. He told me proudly that he hadn't gone in the tub for twenty years and we laughed together, he at the thought of coping without twentieth century living and I at the prospect of a neighbour smelling of Camay soap.

I was caught up in the spirit of my plan. He must go home immediately and throw his dirty clothes over the wall into my yard. I didn't possess a washing machine but I would do them by hand. That Friday night I lined up the soap powders and bleaches with grim satisfaction. I had won the battle! I peeped out of the back door but no clothes appeared over the wall. I must be patient.

Next morning, my two girls came screaming into the bedroom to inform me that something 'nasty' was lying by the backdoor. I hurried downstairs to find to my horror and disgust, several pairs of long johns - men's underwear with full length trousers and sleeves. They hadn't seen the light of day for decades; neither were they even grey in colour. They were filthy black and as the girls so accurately observed, Mr Coleman had not worn a nappy or indeed used a toilet roll, ever!

I snatched the girls inside and slammed the door shut. My victory turned sour. Then we started to laugh and we sat on the kitchen floor, tears of hysteria rolling down our cheeks. What could we do? We became three accomplices in a daring plan. We could lift those beastly objects and drop them into the cow trough to soak. But as my eldest girl pointed out, we might poison the cows. We could burn them or bury them but this would mean replacing them and we had no money. I could ask Mr Coleman for some of the hundreds of notes, but that meant defeat for me. There was only one answer - they would have to be washed.

Slowly we opened the door and peeped out, possibly hoping that they may have been carried away, but no, there they were, awaiting their appointment with the promised cleansing. We lined up an array of buckets and an old tub and filled each receptacle with warm water, soap powder and bleach. Then came the tricky and dangerous part of the procedure. Ordering the girls to stand well away, I poked the garden rake under the offenders and popped each of the six pairs of long johns into the liquid, shutting my eyes as I did so. As they slowly submerged beneath the bubbling liquid, the girls leapt forward with delight and pressed the ancient cloth below the surface with sticks.

Here, the offenders stayed for several days - until the water became icy. Finally, we spilled them onto the yard and examined them. Gloomily we repeated the performance several times until at least we dared to touch them. Then we rinsed them in the cow trough and hung them on the line to dry. Many days later, they were proclaimed clean, but not white. They would remain forever a dismal shade of grey, but clean nevertheless.

Now I must put the second part of my plan into action. Carrying the garments, I visited Mr Coleman and told him quite firmly that he must have a bath and that henceforth he must use a toilet roll. Did he understand my message? Smiling toothily, he seemed strangely content. It was, after all, a Saturday and that appeared to be a good day for a bath. All day long I noted with approval the spirals of steady smoke rising from his chimney. I could imagine the water being heated almost to boiling point. I felt relaxed and calm; I had achieved the impossible.

That evening we paid a visit to Crewe, several miles away, and we returned late. Knowing that our neighbour would not be in bed, and impatient to see the results of my labour, I hurried round in the dark. I could see a light shining from his bathroom window. I knocked on the front door and listened. The silence was overbearing. Then I heard a small trickling sound and looking own I saw to my horror that water was running out under the door. I shouted and hammered on the front door but the house remained silent and locked.

Mr Coleman must have drowned in his bath. I saw it all so vividly, his wizened body floating awkwardly, drifting in a sea of murky Camay scented filth - what had I done! Why, oh why hadn't I left him as he was? I was a murderer, through my own stupid missionary zeal.

Frantically, I ran back for my family and we retraced my footsteps to the door. Everything was as before. It would have to be a matter for the police and what could I say? I felt hysterical. We would make one last effort. The backdoor had yet to be pummelled. Together we beat upon the splintered wood, crying out his name in desperation.

We finally turned away, our hearts full of sadness, when suddenly we heard a noise. The door opened. Mr Coleman stood like a god in the doorway, illuminated by the kitchen light. Steam poured from him in almost liquid form. He was bright pink and had a towel fastened around his waist. His body was fit and strong, not wrinkled and worn. He was a magnificent old man, upright and proud.

Smiling fondly at us, he explained the pleasures of that long and luxurious bath, which had lasted for six hours. Finally, he had fallen asleep in the soapy water. And why were we all crying?
We turned away, too emotional to speak. The scent of pink Camay soap had even drifted as far as our own back yard.

Of course, life continued and our neighbour remained of great interest to us, until tragically he caught pneumonia after falling into a ditch on his return journey from collecting his pension. Here he had lain all day and all night and when he was finally discovered, it was too late to save him.

For me, his finest hour was the emergency that wasn't that resulted from that glorious bath and that is how I will always remember him, an old man whose lifestyle and philosophy was foreign to me; a man of the earth who refused to be influenced by anyone. By allowing himself to be cleansed, he was simply showing us that he loved us and that if this were what it took to prove that love, he would willingly go along with the charade. And for the love he showed us that day, he'll remain forever in my heart.

Becca and the Turkeys

Living in the countryside isn't the same as living from the countryside. It seems to me that so many people aspire to country living but know nothing about the land or what is happening beyond their window. Money may buy them a picturesque cottage but living in it is as shallow and meaningless as a picture postcard. Living from the land is something quite different, particularly if there is no money for washing machines, central heating and glazed windows!

Our lives were taken up by the rhythm of the seasons. We ate from the land; rabbits caught by our ferrets, ducks and wood pigeons shot in the thick woods, mushrooms from the fields, pike from the unfished pools, eggs from our fourteen chickens and all our vegetables from our garden including purple sprouting broccoli. Every morning Robert would collect a huge can of steaming milk fresh from the cows and our girls, plump as butter, would play in the long grass, hiding under giant rhubarb leaves and discovering tiny imaginary people with bumpy legs and thorny hands! They had many imaginary playmates, including one named Lek Lek who sat at dinner with us every night.

Long involved battles between the Roundheads and Cavaliers would take place between them as they fought with sappy sticks and as I watched I wondered about those battles of long ago when the Roundheads marched across the Cheshire countryside. The cow trough would become a deep pool housing ancient treasure, which could only be touched by plunging in deep sticks. In the winter months it froze over, providing a white patterned scribbling pad for them and in the spring they slipped frogspawn into its muddy water.

On dark frosty nights our fox and badger would cross our garden leaving very few tell tale signs of their existence. Our hens were safely locked up for the night and our Clumber spaniel, kennelled in the old pigsty, would let us know of their passing. One Christmas we bought turkeys to rear and fatten and kept them at the bottom of the garden where they ate their way towards their fate on the Christmas dinner table. My eldest daughter, who was in charge of the hens, took it upon herself to be guardian of these huge wattled birds and would regularly visit them - even when she appeared to be the smallest one in their pen. One night she heard Robert talking about their safety as a huge rat had made a home below their cote, probably because of their body warmth.

That same night she announced that she was going to sleep with the turkeys in order to protect them from the nasty rat. I was terrified for her safety as by now they weighed on average twenty pounds each and there were twenty birds altogether. I had visions of my little girl being pecked to death, frozen to death or bitten by the legendary rat. But Robert insisted that she should do as she wished and down she went at dusk when they had settled down in their cote for the night. She was warmly dressed, but wouldn't take a torch and I wondered at her bravery. I spent most of the night awake, even though her little sister had tried to reassure me.

"Don't worry Mummy. Becca sings to them and they tell her gobbly gobbly stories and they are Becca's friends."

At dawn I crept to the end of the garden through the hoar frost. I could see the footprints of the fox as he had silently slipped through the hedge. The wood pigeons were cooing softly and smoke rose from Mr Coleman's cottage. Otherwise all was still. For a brief moment I paused before lifting the latch on the wooden door, and heart pounding I peered inside. Warm air rushed to meet me and twenty pairs of beady eyes watched me warily. Cradled in their midst, lying on a soft bed of living down lay Becca, fast asleep. Quietly I closed the door, returning to our cottage to light the fire. An hour later Becca walked in having collected the hens' eggs and proceeded to get ready for school. Reassured that they were quite safe as the rat couldn't creep up through the floorboards and no predator could enter their warm home, she felt no need to repeat her vigil.

I'm sure country living had a lot to do with turning Becca into the strong woman she became. Maybe it all started with befriending a community pariah and defending her defenceless turkeys. But despite how much we had embraced the country life, needless to say, we never ate a single one of those turkeys for Christmas and they were sold at the Beeston auction.

The Dinner Lady

I first became aware of her when I called at the little country school early in the mornings to drop off my two small girls before travelling on to Crewe, where I was working. It was a hurried affair as I also had to deposit my son with his child minder in Crewe, so I rarely had time to socialise like many of the local young mothers. My girls brought her to my attention long before I had ever met her.

They had often queried my profession as a schoolteacher, work that always seemed to be associated with tension and rushing from place to place. One autumn day, as we were driving home to our cottage at Beeston, my eldest daughter asked me quite bluntly why I didn't surrender all claims to teaching and take up the infinitely superior work of a dinner lady and school cleaner. As we drove through the autumnal Cheshire lanes strewn with the year's dying leaves, she leant over to the front seat and questioned my dedication, pointing out the highly esteemed human qualities both girls had generously bestowed upon Mrs Dean. From the back seat of the car came the second opinion, oiced by my four year old, anxious to support her big sister in this important matter.

Autumn blew into winter, and we battled the roads to education, driving through icy weather and dark evenings. I felt reassured when I returned late to pick up the girls, as I knew that their much-loved school became a warm harbour of safety against the winter gales and icy conditions. The assembly room boasted an open fire and I often found the girls playing happily in a warm shadowy room as Mrs Dean swept and dusted away the debris of the day's learning. Their friendship was firmly established and I realised, with some dismay, that they may have been right and I most probably had chosen the wrong profession.

My son began to toddle and the carrycot changed to a car seat. He was a sturdy, lively child, who quickly outgrew his small sister. He loved to arrive back at the little school and would quickly invade their peace. Tolerant, loving and gentle, they would sweep him up in their small arms, a large cuckoo in a small nest, and show him the artistic offerings pinned to the walls.

I would chat to Mrs Dean and she would discuss the school's busy day. She was a round, comfortable looking lady with red cheeks and greying hair. Her blue eyes twinkled, never betraying even the smallest sign of past unhappiness. She lived in a tithed cottage as we did, and our bond was formed through that umbilical thread to the Tollmache estate. We were remnants of a medieval age, tenants to a lord, with all its connotations of bowing, gratefulness and fear of losing our homes.

I remember laughingly telling her the story of Lord Tollmache, who flew in with the swallows one day in May to inspect us, his new tenants. His winters were spent in France; he lived only with the gentle elements of England, enjoying the summer in his castle. I was quick to point out my new baby son but he replied that he was far more interested in dogs and, in particular, our clumber spaniel. Then he was gone, roaring up the lane in his Rolls Royce.

Mrs Dean exchanged stories that went far back into her lifetime. She had always been a tenant on the estate and knew well the changeable and fickle nature of her powerful landlords. She was conditioned by an ancient feudal system into submission, even emerging with dignity. She knew 'her place' and was happy to live out her life on the small piece of borrowed land. Or so I thought at that time.

Becca and Rachel on the railing, Francis in foreground.
Beeston, 1974

One day in June, my trundling toddler sought the outdoors. Forsaking the assembly hall, which was heavy with the scents of foxgloves, primroses and wild daffodils, he popped out into the late spring sunshine and made his way to the swings. His two gentle sisters anxiously pursued him, calling out frantically, but he continued in a straight line, resembling a beagle following the scent of children who had long gone home. Mrs Dean and I watched from the door as his fragile sisters helped him onto a swing – one pushed him and the other one waited to catch him.

It was all over in a flash. Down he went, one heavy bundle of arms, legs and nappy to crash on to the hard ground. His new top teeth hung by shreds of thin flesh from his gum, his wails shook the rooks from the tall oak trees and his two pale-faced sisters were white-faced with guilt and horror. I found calm and wonderful support in our friend, the dinner lady. Quickly, but calmly, she picked up the screaming blood covered child, holding his mouth with the corner of her pinafore. I was later to find that she was also holding his teeth in, a quick action, which saved them. We drove back to Crewe to a dentist and following successful treatment, we returned again to the scene of the accident where I dropped her off several hours later to complete her chores.

Summer turned again into autumn and the girls were anxious to return to their school. My eldest girl now sat, proud and isolated, in an advanced class, having read everything in the school, including the headmaster's private scribblings, much to his annoyance. Her sister, a fairy child adored by all, would continue to play.

Mrs Dean had also returned but she was different - animated, even excited. Some great event had stirred her soul and she was waiting out in the car park that evening to tell me. She had been a widow for a number of years; her husband had fallen from the roof of their tithe cottage and broken his back and she had devoted years to nursing him until his death. An invitation to spend a summer holiday in Scotland with a cousin had charmed her away from her native Cheshire for the first time since her honeymoon many years ago.

During the holiday she had been introduced to a Scottish gentleman, a widower who had entertained and wooed her. Minus the pinafore and with new clothes and a perm, Mrs Dean allowed herself to be totally captivated by this charming man. She could hardly believe that he could be interested in her, but within days of her return to Cheshire a letter came through the post from Scotland. It was a liaison in the making. I congratulated her, pondering on what passions and dreams may be behind that rosy well-worn face. But she was sad. Something was not right. She thrust the letter into my hands demanding my inclusion in the intrigue.

It was a beautifully written letter, scribed lovingly with an ink pen onto pale grey unlined paper. Grammatically it was a work of art. The Glasgow gentleman was once a Glasgow grammar school boy steeped in Keats and Shelley. His letter flowed from present into future. He had found the lady of his dreams; he was her knight in shining armour. His words wooed her subtly and firmly. He left no question in his words. At seventy years of age, he was confident in his ardour.

Yet, at the same time, he was entirely respectful, dignified and gentle.

I placed the letter gently back into the well-worn hands. Then she voiced her worst nightmare. "I can't write."

For several minutes we stood together in the weak autumn sunshine, such good friends, yet separated by three decades and by education, which on the one hand liberated me and on the other hand had imprisoned her.

The enormity of her social inadequacy swamped her. Tears rolled down her cheeks and her body shook; such sadness overcame her that I took her in my arms and we clung together bereft at the tragic circumstances. I felt that these tears had fallen before in other playgrounds many years ago before she was removed at the age of nine to polish silver for the gentry.

I felt anger. We must do something, but what? Then I knew. I would become her pen, her literacy. She would dictate her deepest thoughts and I would pour them onto paper, which would wing its way to Glasgow and her loved one. It seemed the natural thing to do.

We discussed every detail of our plan. We decided upon a trial letter that would be written that very night. I would hand it over the following morning and Mrs Dean would copy it. She desperately wanted to try out handwriting that had lain dusty and obsolete within her for over fifty years.

The following evening she was waiting in the assembly hall, hands slightly trembling as she dusted and cleaned. She handed me her copy of the letter. With dismay I looked at the writing of a four year old. Briskly, I reassured her. I would write the letters and she would sign them.

That night, sitting by a log fire with all three children tucked up in bed, I wrote that first letter, on Basildon Bond pale blue unlined paper, and with an ink pen. It was joyful but reticent, replying to all the suggestions of the grey letter. It was the beginnings of a refined and gentle courtship. Mrs Dean had instructed me on the general content but requested that I put words together without her assistance. So, as I sat and wrote the letter in the living room of the little tithe cottage by the light of the fire, the lover dreamed away in her tithe cottage a few miles away, such dreams that she had not experienced since she was a beautiful young woman of eighteen.

The following morning I gave her the letter and that evening I asked her opinion. She was delighted. The words were worthy of her Scottish gentleman but would I please sign her name, as her writing would not be appropriate. It was not long before the second of a hundred letters hurried down from Scotland. The seasons changed and with them the contents of the letters.

He wrote of such tender moments in his past, his relationship with his mother, his cruel father, his fear of the church, which had inhibited him all his life, and of his frail wife who had been a child and remained so throughout their loveless and childless marriage. He wrote of the highlands and his loyalty to Scotland, even during the freezing winters when snowdrifts almost prevented him from making his way to the post-box. I wrote of Cheshire, the school, my work as a dinner lady and my lonely planned life in my cottage.

I questioned Mrs Dean on her married life and wrote openly about my kind husband who had suffered so much, following the accident. I took poetic liberty, describing Cheshire in the spring when one became intoxicated on the perfumes of the wildflowers. We touched on poetry and I introduced him to Shelley, whilst he introduced me to Mr Milton. As the letter writing grew, his passion grew also. Mrs Dean had regular perms. Indeed she now wore her best nylons and Sunday clothes for school and the wrap-over pinafore disappeared. She was a loved and happy woman.

Mention was made of a visit and the following summer a trip was made yet again to Glasgow, where Mrs Dean's cousin provided a chaperone and her home a haven where many meetings took place. Upon her return, Mrs Dean told me of walks in the park, tea and scones in teahouses where ladies wore gloves and of gentle kisses before her beloved gentleman took leave.

Then, one day, shortly after this visit, word came from Scotland of marriage plans. There must be no delay. He loved her so much. She would marry and move into his home, leaving behind all her ties and subordination to aristocracy. Mrs Dean was ecstatic. She would leave the cottage, the school and even the graveside of her husband. It would be flowerless but she must go despite everything. I felt a pang of sadness, even loneliness. We would miss her, but she deserved such love and companionship.

The school holidays arrived and I did not see Mrs Dean for two weeks. When I drove into the schoolyard I knew a decision had been made, but I was shocked to find that she was about to decline his offer and end the relationship. Why, I questioned, sensing the agony within her.

The wedding plans had been laid, the church booked and a small reception planned. In his letter, our Scottish gentleman described the joy of signing the register together. He longed for the moment when their two signatures rested together for eternity on paper, to be witnessed by all.

The secret would be out! The large handwriting would betray all that had gone before. She could not go through with it. I was devastated! I begged,

I pleaded with her. I offered to take a train to Scotland and explain everything, but her mind was made up. She asked me to write a final letter ending the friendship forever and asking that there should be no replies.

That night I wept over the letter, attempted again and again to write those final words. Finally, I did so but with the licence Mrs Dean had bestowed upon me I declared my love but wrote of my impossible situation in Cheshire. All my memories rested here; my husband's grave, my little cottage, my childhood. I could not betray my entire life, uproot and leave behind my beloved county.

And so it ended. Such a passion and love between two old people. Mrs Dean returned to her crossover pinafores and her ritual cleaning of the school. Our friendship resumed its easy relationship. Only I ever knew of the passion and longing in our dinner lady and her unrequited love.

CHESHIRE, Beeston

Chapter Six:

The Call of the Sea 1974 - 1980

Nets on a Cheshire Field

One winter day when I returned from work, I was amazed to see Robert pulling something along in the field opposite Dean Bank Cottage. Feeling curious, the girls and I crossed the road and treading carefully over the cattle grid we walked towards what looked like ropes lying in the grass. Robert grinned, looking extremely pleased with himself.

"These," he announced knowledgeably, "Are fishing nets."

The girls ran about in the field, spreading the entwined nets out on the grass and pulling weed from them. "What for?"

"For the boat."

"What boat?"

"The one we are going to buy."

I looked around at the flat grassy meadows in a county that was about as far away from the sea as you could get. There was simply no answer to this, so we went inside with talk of boats and the sea and I realised with astonishment that the boy at Blackpool, the man who had sailed around the world at sixteen and the man who milked the cows were all standing side by side and very close together! Robert was married to the sea and little did I know what great adventures lay ahead as we dreamed of an angler's boat and how to save the money.

My teaching took on urgency and I made myself available for relief work at the primary school near to the childminder who looked after our son. My classroom resembled the seabed on one wall and across the other wall were the fishing nets, borrowed for a project on conservation and pollution of our oceans. Both at home and at work, the sea called us. We would make hurried trips into Wales and once we travelled as far as Fowey in Cornwall to visit Robert's closest friend, Roger Dunn, who was the pilot for Par Harbour. Robert had worked as a boatman for him when he had finished in the Merchant Navy and the two men shared many hair-raising memories of their work together.

We were looking for a boat similar to those that took out anglers from Mevagissey, in Cornwall; well-built rounded little boats called Mevagissey Toshers. With luck one may be working out of North Wales and in the meantime we saved. One spring day Robert discovered his boat at Deganwy, which is near to Conwy and from there, he eventually took out his first party of anglers. He drove from Beeston before dawn to arrive at the little boat in which we had invested all our savings. She was named *Vydal* and eventually Robert sailed her round to Holyhead, which was where we had decided to fish from.

In going to Anglesey, we weren't to know that there would two fishing boats in our lives. First would be *Vydal* and then *Our Venture*.

I was given the arduous task of finding somewhere to live and together the children and I searched for a cottage, which we hoped to buy with a 100% mortgage from the local council. Eventually we found one near to the sea in an area named Porth-y-Felin. It was one of a number of small cottages built originally for the men who constructed the breakwater. *Vydal* could be moored in the harbour and we simply had to walk down the road, under the bridge and across to the beach to check her safety. Robert moored his dinghy here and started advertising for anglers.

Welsh living was very different from our lives in the Cheshire countryside. The Welsh language was and still is of great importance in North Wales and when I enrolled my girls in the local primary school, I was told that they would be receiving Welsh lessons as part of the compulsory curriculum. They settled in happily and our lives took on a different beat.

During the years that we lived in Holyhead, we experienced the growing up of our three children, the effects of the capricious weather that influenced Robert's angling business, the Welsh education of our three children and the lasting effect of the Welsh community on our lives. Then there were the hidden influences, the ghosts of Anglesey, forever present even on a bright sunny day. You only had to look up at Holyhead Mountain to the shadows and the mist to realise that the past was always present in the very rocks and earth of this ancient land.

It is no coincidence that Holyhead has remained virtually unchanged since we lived there. There are the obvious signs such as its people, many of whom still occupy their original houses that we visited when we lived there and the teachers, many of whom are still in the schools where I taught and where my children were educated. This subtle continuity is best explained by the following incident. When I returned to Holyhead years later, I called in on the children's Primary school to tell the teachers about my now grown children's progress. I entered the hall and sitting around a table were the dinner ladies, eating their lunch, as it was now afternoon and the pupils were back in their classes. When I told them that my son was now six foot, six inches tall, one of the dinner ladies laughed and said, "We always thought he would be a big boy. Many a time he used to have six puddings following a large dinner!" Everyone laughed and I was astonished that she was still there, speaking as if it were yesterday!

The lasting signs that define its heritage and culture are subtle, the stone walls with the same gaps, the well trodden paths to the quarry and Primrose Hill where those namesake flowers show their yellow heads for a few short days, the well trodden ancient paths to the quarry and beyond and the grey houses whose occupants live on bringing up their children in that rich but inevitably unchanging existence. In all other places I have observed changes but not so in North Wales, where the ancient land defies that modern day obsession – destruction of a community.

I sense that my entire family were influenced and caught in this Celtic spell that weaves its intangible threads around all those who choose to live out part or the whole of their lives on this Holy Island to which I am drawn back again and again.

Making friends

We became part of the Welsh community only after an initial battle. Robert first met Glyn Shergo, a local fisherman in the 'The Vic', a local pub a few doors up from our cottage, and frequented by fishermen.

At dawn of the same day, Robert and I had been out beyond the breakwater in our first boat, Vydal. We laid our nets for salmon but that day we returned to find only several silver scales clinging them.

Robert accused Glyn of stealing salmon from his nets as that morning he had seen Glyn's dinghy as he rowed silently in the mist, lifting and checking his own nets. Glyn turned on him immediately and the two men battled verbally.

Robert said that he would steal from Glyn's nets if he stole from ours.

A silent Welsh audience observed this confrontation but through this angry incident respect grew between the two young men and they became best friends, recognising the same strengths and qualities in each other.

Later that week as we floated silently along an unusually glassy surface in our dinghy to check our nets, we found our culprit. Headless salmon littered our nets, bitten clean in two. And finally the lifeless body of a young seal, which we sadly released to the sea.

The False Teeth

One day two of Robert's brothers, who worked at the Rolls Royce factory in Crewe, phoned up to ask if they could bring several Rolls Royce old age pensioners fishing. Robert took them out into the bay in reasonable weather. There was a faint swell as they hooked into spur dog (small shark). As Robert cleaned and gutted the fish, hosing down the deck, one old man was violently seasick over the side and lost his false teeth.

Another old man sneaked up to Robert and removing his own false teeth, he suggested that Robert tell the first old man that he'd found his teeth inside one of the fish, which must have swallowed them. Robert did this and the old man tried the teeth, said "Oh no, they're not mine," and threw them over the side! A fight broke out and the two old men had to be separated. One was placed at the stern and one at the bow! Robert's brothers said that they would have to be separated on the coach during the return journey!

Now lying on the seabed are two sets of false teeth, but upon hearing the story my children were all convinced that fish would be wearing them!

HOLYHEAD BREAKWATER

Another Kind of Resident

I heard stories of a great conger eel that lived deep inside the wreck of an old steamship named "The Orian." It had established itself so well and had grown to be so huge that it trapped itself forever inside the wreck. It lay in wait for passing fish, and divers had seen its green smooth head and large watery eyes. They knew only too well to avoid the wreck as the conger eel could bite and twist a man's arm off.

Prince on the Beach

One day a young prince stepped ashore at Holyhead. His ship, the H.M.S. Bronington was moored in the harbour alongside two sister ships. They were mine sweepers on an exercise spotting and charting mines. Rumours swept the small town; the man born to be king would drink at the sailing club and meet the locals. The first I knew of it was noting strangers who arrived in advance of the Royal Navy to check the beaches and the port. Security become noticeable only to the locals, then one day the strangers arrived.

From time to time over the next few days I would hear local gossip. Prince Charles had been spotted going into the sailing club. He had been seen in the navy launch, and a local barmaid had served him a drink. I would walk along Stoney beach to check on *Vydal*, which we tied up at the old jetty and I would point out the Navy mine sweepers moored in the harbour to my children.

PORTH-Y-FELIN, HOLYHEAD

One night I mentioned to Robert that I would like to see Prince Charles as I was not at all convinced that he was with the Navy ships out there. Robert burst out laughing and told me that every night during the entire visit the launch had moored alongside *Vydal* and Charles had stepped ashore across our boat. His detective had sworn Robert to secrecy, as this was the safest point for Charles to come ashore. McKenzie Jetty was for too obvious a landing place and an even more obvious IRA target. He'd chatted to Charles on several occasions. If I really wanted to meet him I needed to go down on my own and wait on Stoney Beach at 9pm that night. It was a warm summer evening and didn't grow dark until after ten.

I left the cottage and slowly wandered down to the sea, wondering whether Robert was playing a joke on me or not. I passed Sandy on the way and he gave me a cheery wave as he strode up the hill towards his own cottage, solitary and self-contained as always. My thin shoes trod the gravelled paths and the warm evening sun spilled across the habour, causing the masts of the yachts to gleam. As always the air was filled by the continuous unearthly tinkling sound of the rigging attached to the masts. They rattled in the wind, which invariably blew. My father used to call the place 'Windy Head', aptly named for most days of the year.

Walking past the Sailing club I turned left towards the secluded beach. A slight wind blew against my loose brown dress, one which had served me during the arduous seven months of pregnancy with my son, but which I still wore as I loved the memories associated with it. I was hardly fit to meet a prince! I smiled to myself but at the same time couldn't help feeling anxious. Was I the only commoner in history to meet a prince on this stretch of beach? Maybe it had occurred before, hundred of years ago? Certainly it did not seem a strange thing to be doing.

Nothing moved. *Vydal* was expertly tried to the jetty, the rowing boats were pulled up on the shingle and the seagulls had drifted away, no longer attracted by fishing catches. That clear bright light which comes before dusk and throws long shadows across the earth lit up the harbour. I knew why the Welsh loved, fought and cared for their land - it was very beautiful. Holyhead Mountain looked enticing, hiding North Stack lighthouse and those evil tides that ripped around its base. I felt very content. My family had feasted on lobster, crab, whiting, and conger eel fresh from the day's catch.

Suddenly I felt rather foolish. Why did I want to meet Charles? It was certainly nothing to do with my ego. No one would know!

This island with all its pagan and Christian religion seemed to be the appropriate stage on which to meet a prince, who for a brief moment in time, would step from the pages of history. Later I would see his image on television and in newspaper and smile to myself for I had met him, and thus behind him then all the kings and queens of England. He was after all Prince of Wales. I remembered that Welsh ceremony that had proclaimed him Prince of Wales.

Married to my first husband, fresh from university, we were caught innocently catching salmon from a Welsh stream on that very day, and heavily fined!

My thoughts interrupted, I heard distant voices and sure enough the Royal Navy launch approached, filled with young sailors. I stepped back into the shadows of the old lifeboat hut and watched as they piled out of the launch, which floated onto the wooden ramp at Trinity House jetty. At least twenty young men clambered out on to the beach. Climbing the steps, they wandered off to the sailing club, the sound of their voices growing fainter and fainter. Suddenly two young men appeared high above me on the old jetty. They seemed relaxed and chatted together as they climbed down and walked across the shingled beach. I watched them from the shadows. One man was in his forties and wearing a suit. The other one was younger, much younger and quite slightly built. In height he was about five feet ten inches and wearing slacks and a navy jacket. He suddenly threw back his head and laughed and I realised with a shock that I was standing within twelve feet of a prince!

Stepping forward into the last of the sun's rays I spoke. Both men were startled as neither had spotted me. The suited man stepped in front of Charles glancing around nervously but I smiled again and introduced myself. Pointing over to Vydal I explained that we owned the boat and that I was completely on my own. I approached Charles and the detective allowed himself a small smile and edged away slightly. I stood on the beach facing the prince. He stared at me. He was very young, maybe eight or nine years younger than me. His hair was thick but neat. He had laughing eyes and when he spoke I hardly detected the pronounced southern English accent that would develop later in his life.

So we began a lively conversation, which would last for at least half an hour. We talked about many things; Holyhead, Wales, the Welsh language, the Irish Sea and he questioned me about my life as both mother and teacher. Twice he asked me how I managed to look after three small children and also work. He laughed when I told him some of the problems. He asked me to describe one of our evening meals and how did Robert prepare the variety of fish that we ate? At one point the detective strolled over and asked me if I realised how fortunate I was to have all this time in conversation, but Charles simply waved him away and carried on talking.

By now the sun had gone down and dusk was settling around us, turning all the fishing boats and yachts into solid shapes and finally into dark outlines against the sea. Still we talked, when suddenly we hard a tinkling noise as liquid hid the stones from a great height. Charles turned around, laughing loudly.

One of the returning sailors was peeing off the end of the jetty about twenty feet above us silhouetted against the lights from the launch.

Turning, Charles shouted, "Lower the lights coxon, lady present!"

We all burst out laughing, and then it was time to board the liberty launch that would ferry the sailors back to The Bronington. I said goodbye to Charles, who invited the sailors to board his launch. They all piled on board and the launch actually touched the bottom and gravelled to a halt. Charles and the men piled out and together we all began to push. I remember looking down at his hand, next to mine on the bow, so unlike the working hands of many of the men that I have known. Finally they were afloat and Charles leaned over the side of the launch and thanked me, first for talking to him so honestly and secondly for helping to push the boat.

"Here take this," he said, pushing a six-pack of lager into my hands! Then they were off, growing smaller and smaller until they disappeared into the darkness.

Clutching my present, I wandered home wondering about the entire incident. I placed the lager on the kitchen shelf as a memory and it wasn't until two years later that I discovered each tin was empty. Robert had consumed the lot and carefully replaced the cans!

A few days after my meeting on the beach, Robert brought home Charles' navigating officer, an extremely pleasant young man who stayed to tea with us and entertained the children. Robert suggested to him that the bay contained many wrecks and reefs and it seemed obvious that a smart officer would lay mines where they would be hard to detect, in other words, next to wrecks and reefs.

The following evening when we met him again he confirmed that The Bronington had found three mines, all discovered where he had been advised to look. Suddenly the exercise was over and overnight all three minesweepers left.

I have often reflected on that meeting, trying to place it in perspective. I spoke to a very pleasant easygoing young man who had yet to face the growing responsibilities of heritage. Finally he rests in my mind as just yet another person in a long line of people who came and went from that mystical place, Holy Island.

BOL SACH, HOLYHEAD

Our Venture

In our home is a little ashtray. No one would give it a second glance as it sits on a small table next to Robert's chair. Rolled cigarette ends continually fill it and each day I tenderly pick it up and empty away its debris. Around the outside of the pot are painted the words 'Our Venture' and printed on its clay side is a tiny blue trawler.

It is the only visual memory of an incredible boat, which carried forth two strong men and delivered them into the arms of the sea. God, in his omnipotence, thought otherwise and gave them back their lives. I want to tell you a sea story that is lived and re-lived in the hearts of these two men, but to fully understand it; I need to explain their friendship with each other.

Robert achieved his childhood ambition to go to sea and has been subject to its whims and powers ever since. The Dunn family had been involved with the sea for generations. Automatically Roger would follow in his father's footsteps and his son would follow him. Roger Dunn piloted ships from Par for forty-three years. Now in his sixties, he remains the strongest man I know. He doesn't drink or smoke, believes in the Jewish religion and has the most incredible laugh.

Fate drew the two men together in their youth; one who had known the ocean all his life and the other from land-locked Cheshire with a calling for the sea, a dreamer and a wanderer. Their friendship is a lasting one and I became part of it. My children love Roger and he is a permanent part of their lives.

When we moved to Holyhead from Cheshire, *Vydal* was chosen as our first boat because Robert recognized her seaworthiness through his work in Cornwall. During a great December storm, two years after we had settled in Holyhead, she was lost, and as we stood on Stony Beach and watched her slowly sinking out on her moorings, little did we know that our next boat would change all our lives forever.

With the £1000 insurance money and our savings of £1200, Robert set off with his friend Billy Edwards to travel as far as Scotland to look for a trawler. He drove our V.W. Beetle and reached as far as Mallaig. Finally, he and Billy returned home to our cottage in Holyhead, exhausted and disappointed. We simply did not have enough money for the boats he had seen.

That night, recovering from the long journey, Robert looked despondently through 'The Fishing News'. Suddenly he closed the paper and told me that he was off to Hayle in Cornwall! He only stayed long enough to discuss his plans with his friend Sandy Balfour and then he was gone, carrying £600 for a deposit.

He told me that after driving all night, he arrived at Hayle to discover a forty-five foot German trawler named *Our Venture*, which was resting against the quay. Her planks were two and a quarter inch oak and she was built in 1958 on the River Rhine and was fitted with a Deutsche engine. The estuary revealed mud flats as the tide was out and early that November morning he scrutinized the beautifully shaped boat and knew that she was for him.

He had arranged to see the owner, who turned up at eight o'clock to see a very weary dishevelled young man, looking thoughtfully down at the boat on her mooring. We will never know what thoughts the owner had but Robert's enthusiasm and dreams certainly affected him, for he agreed to let *Our Venture* go for what Robert could pay, even though she was worth much more. Robert could scarcely believe his luck. He made two phone calls, one to me and one to Roger, his old friend at Par, Cornwall.

That evening he and Roger met up once again and excitedly discussed the trawler. The next morning they drove to Hayle where Roger confirmed Robert's thoughts. She was, in Roger's words, "'andsome, Bob, 'andsome".

So began plans to bring her back to Holyhead through some of the most treacherous seas in the world, for she had to sail across that part of the Atlantic where it meets the Irish Sea. Food was taken on board, including several pots of honey from Roger's bees, navigation charts and a Bible. Five hundred gallons of diesel, worth £280, was poured into the tanks.

The quay in Hayle was stacked with huge steel girders, which lay within ten yards of the boat. Robert wondered if the metal had affected the compass but Roger didn't think so.

Both men checked the weather forecast with BBC shipping, the R.A.F. and the meteorological office. 'Maximum force five for the next twenty-four hours.'

Midnight saw *Our Venture* sailing on a full tide, the moon lighting up the estuary as the little boat slipped over the sandbar and out into the Atlantic Ocean. The voyage had begun.

There was a feeling of excitement as they headed out to sea, Roger commenting on the boat's smooth passage and noting that she handled extremely well.

Two or three hours out of Hayle, Roger discovered that the return fuel system wasn't working and he spent an hour altering and designing a system for fuel to go back smoothly into the fuel tanks. Watching Roger in the engine room, Robert could see that he was seasick, yet he continued to fix the fuel system while vomiting at the same time! His brilliant engineering skills did the trick and he was soon back in the wheelhouse, laughing and joking.

Robert recalled telling Shergo, his fishing friend from Holyhead, that he wanted a decked-in boat that the sea could wash over. *Vydal*, his previous boat, had not been closed in.

Seven and a half hours of smooth sailing brought them close to a huge Russian stern trawler, at least three to four hundred feet long and three thousand tons in weight. The men asked for a compass bearing and soon the Russian trawler was a mere dot on the horizon.

Daylight finally came; revealing a dark, wintry December sky and Robert mentioned to Roger that he'd never seen such confused, moody skies and strange winds flying in all directions. Within an hour the wind freshened and began to blow from the southeast. It was behind them and insidiously began to build up a threatening sea. The men dismissed it, both rationalizing that the change of tide and the worst part of the day was upon them. It could only improve and they reassured themselves with the promising weather forecast.

Robert went forward to the cabin to make mugs of tea and as he staggered back across the deck, the wind whipped the drink away into the sea spray. Gradually, throughout the day the waves increased and suddenly they were sailing in gale force winds. The engine was running well and at full revs. Roger went below to oil the rockers, shouting out to Robert that Deutsche engines were wonderful and the boat was 'running 'andsome'.

By four o'clock that afternoon they sailed into a heavy gale, which was full on the stern, pushing the little blue trawler into a running sea. The waves were very heavy, plunging the propeller in and out of the water. Both men discussed how the hell the forecast could be so wrong. The little trawler sailed on, into a pitch-black night and a howling gale and in the blackness, the wind seemed to increase and the seas built up.

Trying to steer to the compass was extremely difficult as she was pushed in another direction. The small light in the wheelhouse and the compass light lit up the faces of the two silent men as they ate dry biscuits, the only food they had in the cabin. The wind began to whistle and the waves behind them changed into cracking seas. The decks were now awash all the time. Immediately outside the wheelhouse was the engine vent, which they turned to stop the sea going into the engine room.

Robert went out to work the whale pump (hand pump) as *Our Venture* had taken some seas. The sea and wind increased into madness! Robert and Roger could never recall such conditions. It was as if the elements had conspired against them, totally controlling their voyage. The boat was running on one sea whilst another one cracked behind them, completely submerging the decks, the bow - everything!

For the first time Robert felt a knot of fear tighten in his stomach. He looked at the implacable Roger on the steering wheel, and both men commented on the ferocity of the sea and wind.

Then the boat burst out of the waves as if gasping for air and within five minutes, another sea hit them, taking them sideways down a thirty-foot wave. The boat straightened up before they hit the trough and both men marvelled at the strength of the little trawler. However, there was to be no respite. The next sea picked them up like a surfboard and with a terrible realisation; they both knew that it wasn't an odd wave any more. The entire sea and winds had combined to a force ten hurricane!

And now Robert must tell you the rest of this story.

I said to Roger, "You know, Rog, they said it would be a force five, but right now it's blowing double that into a hurricane!"

The wind was howling and the seas cracked before they hit us. I recall being on the wheel, I was trying to steer and the compass flipped over and remained upside down. A huge sea hit us, pushed us sideways and turned us around to face head on into the sea. Black cracking waves forty feet high flung spray everywhere. We tried to look at the chart and almanac, thinking we were off the Welsh coast.

Roger grew short tempered because he couldn't find the landmarks. The hurricane took us where it wanted to, flinging us into the huge seas and totally off course. I remembered that I had a distress radio on board and made a call. There was no answer and I realised that no one could hear us.

I distinctly remember lurching out of the wheelhouse to check the mizzenmast at the stern. The wind and rain had plucked the stitching from the mizzen, which was reefed.

Before we had sailed from Hayle, I fastened a rope from the wheelhouse to the forward accommodation. I had tied it to the derrick wire as a precaution, never thinking we'd need it.

Both of us were in the wheelhouse with the door shut, when I noticed the anchor sliding about on the forward deck. We knew that it was tied to a bollard but we could see that the nine feet of attached chain was sliding across the deck.

My fear was that the anchor would fly over the side and smash a hole in the boat and Roger agreed with me. I waited a short while, and then decided that I must secure it or we would be in real trouble.

I tried to find a break in the seas coming over the boat, grabbing hold of the safety line to get forward when a huge sea broke over us. I hung on to the line but the weight of the sea catapulted me like an arrow from the boat. My arm and leg hit the gunwale, my hands grasping at anything or nothing and I was gone!

The shock of the iciness of the sea took my breath away. I didn't know where the surface was. Even though it was between eleven and twelve midnight and pitch-black I could see my air bubbles, and when I exhaled I followed the bubbles - it was the only way I knew whether I was going down or up!

When I burst out of the foam, I could just see the stern of the boat disappearing on the next wave. I had never experienced such coldness. Suddenly, I was picked up in another sea, then began a battle to keep my head above the surface.

My heavy clothing dragged me under. It took all my energy to keep my head above water for the waves were fifty foot high and all I could hear was the continuous screaming of the wind.

'Oh God,' I said, 'don't let me die like this.'

I surfaced; and I saw the back of the boat. I thought, 'that's it! It's all over,' but I didn't want to give in. I struggled and fought, for I was very fit and strong.

Suddenly, like magic, all the dark clouds disappeared! The wind was still hurricane force but there was a full moon! I could see clouds fly past like fighter jets and heard Roger's voice far away, 'I can see you, Bob,' even amongst the screams of the wind. I could see the boat coming on the wave behind me, not in front of me!

She was within twenty-five yards of me, on the same sea! I swam as hard as I could with every ounce of remaining energy to reach her. I actually thought that if I could just get aboard the boat, it wouldn't prove to be the nightmare I had previously felt it was.

I remember my hands grabbing the gunwale as she rolled, part lifting me out of the water, then dumping me back into the icy sea, but I hung on. I knew that being rescued in these conditions was a million to one chance.

Roger rushed out of the wheelhouse, dived on his hands and knees and grasped my belt under my coat. 'I've got you, Bob,' he yelled.

As soon as he'd grabbed hold of me, I tried to yell, 'Roger, let me go, I've had enough.' My mouth was iced up.

I was so exhausted that I thought if I could just put my head under the water, I'd go to sleep.

Suddenly a big loud Cornish voice yelled at me, 'What would I tell Janice?'

At the next roll of the boat, Roger swung me aboard. He rushed inside the wheelhouse as big seas swamped the deck, and put her head into the sea. I crawled into the wheelhouse and he shouted, 'Try shut the door, try shut the door!'

I sat on the seat, holding tightly onto the two handrails. Roger turned to me, 'Bob, take the wet clothes off.'

'I must keep my wet clothes on. I'll die if I take them off'. I knew it was hypothermia. I kept thinking of the survival course I'd done in Anglesey and being told to keep wet clothes on.

Rog pointed out that the anchor had jammed itself between the ribs on the foredeck. It was no longer a threat. After ten minutes of sitting in the corner and watching Rog fighting the wheel to keep us head on into the seas, I was desperate for a smoke. In my thermal jacket under my overcoat was my tobacco. I took it out but it was totally full of seawater. I knew there was no other smoke on the boat and Rog could see I was beginning to crack up.

'Bob, you've got to take the wheel. I'm totally exhausted. I need to lie down, if only for ten minutes.'

'I can't.'

'Give me a break.'

I managed to lift myself up and hung on to the wheel, as a huge sea smashed right over the boat, totally submerging it. By this time the lights had gone and I could smell the batteries gassing under the water, for the engine room was half submerged. Roger tried the whale pump and electric pump with no success.

Roger lay across the wheelhouse, put his hands behind his head and slid to the wheelhouse door and back to the other side of the cabin. His hands protected his head. He stayed in that position for fifteen minutes. Then another huge sea tipped us sideways and Rog was actually standing up on the wheelhouse door!

I shouted, 'Roger, sit in the corner and hang on!'

When he sat in the corner he slipped off one of his Dutch clogs and it was full of blood. His toes were bleeding. I made a silly remark about the need to wear socks and there was a big hearty Cornish laugh.

I hung on to the wheel for twenty minutes whilst Rog sat in the corner, holding onto the handles. Then he took the wheel. I heard him say that he had seen a light and was heading for it but I was too exhausted to look, dozing off instead. I remember waking sharply because the boat had stopped rolling. I rushed up and looked out of the wheelhouse window. To my horror I could see rocks on the left and right hand sides, huge reefs of rocks! Rog couldn't see them. It was pitch-black and he was exhausted.

Sliding the window down, I asked Rog how he'd got there for he'd passed the warning light. Spray flew over the exposed rocks and lashed the boat. He cautiously turned Our Venture around and headed back towards the open seas. I knew that we had run into a reef and told him. He said that I had exceptional eyesight. Then we cleared the light and once again we were in monstrous waves.

After thirty minutes we spotted a big flashing light. It was only when we drew closer that we realised that it was a light ship.

The thought of land gave me some hope. It kept disappearing as another huge sea hit us. We realised that we had been totally turned around. We spotted the light through the back of the wheelhouse window. We turned on top of a sea and headed again to the light. As we drew closer we could read part of the name, the Conningbeg light hhip off Southern Ireland! I had sailed past her many times when I'd been coasting. I thought maybe we could run alongside the Conningbeg, jump onto it and let the boat go. It was the first time in hours that I had felt some hope.

As we sailed really close to the light ship, the Captain came on deck. We were abeam of the Conningbeg and within ten yards when we spotted him, fastened to a lifeline. He screamed to us through a loud hailer, begging us, 'Please keep your distance.' He was terrified we would smash into the light ship or its anchor chains, (they don't have engines). We hailed to him that we were lost and in distress. He hailed back that he would call the Kilmore Quay lifeboat to guide us to port or give us assistance.

We stayed within a hundred yards of the light ship, keeping our head into the sea, continually dropping back and moving up again. After an hour we motored close. The Captain came out on to the deck, shouting that they were on their way. We asked him which way they'd come from. His reply was to point into the hail and spray. I turned to Roger, 'That man is more frightened than us!'

The Captain rushed back in to the safety of his ship. We hurried inside too. I stayed on the wheel, endeavouring to keep Our Venture head on to the sea. At one stage, we were picked up by an enormous wave and sent down sideways. I really thought she'd turn over. We were actually standing on the wheelhouse door! Just before the bottom of the sea, she lifted up!

'I told you these boats don't bang in a big sea!' Rog yelled.

Yet again we turned her round to head into the seas. Two hours seemed like two weeks and we began to lose hope. We hailed the light keeper who told us that the lifeboat had left two hours ago.

An hour later, I thought I saw an orange light, but maybe I was imagining things. I continued to keep a sharp lookout and as we rode on top of a fifty-foot wave, I spotted the orange light again. Forty minutes later it appeared and disappeared. Finally, within thirty yards of us, there appeared a lifeboat with a crew hooked in. Roger hailed that we'd had a man overboard and that he was sick. They instructed us to follow them. They daren't come alongside.

'You just show us the way. We're right, matey,' Rog yelled.

Ten minutes later the life boat hit a massive sea, causing Rog to voice his fears aloud, 'We may end up rescuing them, Bob!' By this time we had a huge amount of confidence in *Our Venture*. We were both concerned for the lifeboat and crew.

In the shelter of the Saltee Islands we were in slightly calmer waters. When we cleared them we were back into huge seas once more. Suddenly, we saw a flashing light at the end of the pier and what appeared to be the breakwater. Huge five cornered jacks made out of concrete provided massive sea breakers. The wind was howling and it was pitch-black, even though it was seven o'clock in the morning. Thirty-one hours had past since we left Hayle!

We were amazed when we came round the end of the breakwater to an anxiously waiting reception of the entire Irish village of Kilmore Quay! Men jumped aboard the boat, moored her up, put fenders down and welcomed us. A doctor, the police, the lifeboat secretary and the remainder of the life boat crew provided a welcoming committee whilst the rest of the villagers stood back, marvelling at the little vessel. They were shocked when they saw how small she was. They'd thought it was a big French trawler in trouble.

The doctor took my pulse immediately and then suggested that we go straight away to the lifeboat secretary's house. I paused and spoke to the policemen.

'Just a minute! Do you smoke? I'm desperate for a cigarette!'

As I inhaled I told him that it was the nicest cigarette I'd ever had in my life! Then two fishermen from the crowd stepped forward quietly, 'did you really get swept over the side in that storm? Did you have a life jacket on?' I told them that I hadn't worn one, and briefly outlined the swim to the boat. Then I overheard a remark from someone in the crowd, 'I told you, Michael, how important it is to learn to swim!'

Several villagers were concerned because Roger had disappeared. One of the men jumped onto *Our Venture*, to peer into the wheelhouse, he could hear Rog shuffling about. He called out and the reply from the engine room made everyone smile.

'I can't come up yet. I've got to pump the bilges and sump out.' For he had found that they were blocked up with old fish scales from her days as a fishing trawler.

The Irish man smiled, 'Jesus, you're a bloody hard man.'

Rog shouted again, 'It's Bob that needs the attention, I'm all right.'

So they took me off to the secretary's house where the doctor pronounced that I wasn't well enough to travel to the Wexford Hospital. I was told to take a warm bath and was soon tucked up in bed with hot water bottles and thick blankets. Once I was in bed, the doctor sat and talked to me, refusing to let me sleep. He asked me many questions about my family to make sure that I had no memory loss. Finally he gave me an injection in my right arm.

I eventually woke up in a darkened room to find Rog sitting by my bed. The wind was still howling but Rog grinned when he saw me open my eyes and jumped up to make me a cuppa. I heard him laughing in the other room, that lovely big Cornish laugh, and then in he came, accompanied by the village priest, the policeman and the lifeboat secretary. They all looked at me then left.

Roger leant forward conspiratorially, saying quietly, 'Bob, they cooked me bacon and eggs and I didn't want to refuse so I ate it. After all this, I'm sure God'll forgive me!' Roger, being Jewish, never ate pork, of course.

I managed to climb out of bed, feeling incredibly weak and cold. Bacon and eggs were cooked for me in the warm kitchen and as I ate, I watched Roger entertaining the Irish gathering with Cornish stories that created big hearty laughter. Soon I was openly shivering again and at the suggestion of the secretary, I returned to a warm bed and slept until 8am the following morning. My entire body ached with the ordeal and my lips were cracked and painful.

Meanwhile, the police had informed everyone of the past events, both in

Holyhead and Cornwall, although the BBC had already checked out the story and broadcast it on television in Welsh. 'Welsh fisherman swept overboard!'

The secretary found me some clothes to put on, and after we'd had breakfast, we visited the individual homes of each lifeboat member. They all commented on the hurricane, telling us that the new self-righting 40-foot lifeboat had been stretched to its limit during the rescue. It was the first time that they'd tried it in extreme weather and told us that it was the worst storm they had ever experienced. They were even more astonished that I had survived in the icy Irish Sea for twenty minutes.

The secretary said to every one of them, 'Now, will this convince you to start the swimming club! Here's your living proof that swimming can save your life!'

That night there had been three ships lost at sea, a thirteen thousand tonner, a three thousand tonner and a fifteen tonner. All disappeared without a trace. *Our Venture* was only a 20-ton beamer and they marvelled at her, for she had carried us through the worst storm in their living memory.

The storm began to die down but the wind continued to blow a force eight and I still couldn't get warm even though I was given every attention. Roger told me that we'd received a phone call from Holyhead to say that a lobster fishing friend of mine, Billy Edwards, was coming across on the ferry to Dublin and driving down to Kilmore Quay to pick us up in his van. Roger had had an offer from a friend in Cornwall to fly him back home, in a helicopter. He refused, saying that he was making sure that 'Bob gets home safe.'

I remember little of the journey for I slept most of the time in the bed made up in the back of the van. We were waved on and off the Irish ferry like celebrities and 'Robert Shephard - Welsh fisherman' was taken home, along with the contraband in the van. They'd loaded it with whisky and cigarettes.

I cried as Billy Edwards' van pulled up outside our little home and Robert climbed out. He was barely recognisable and didn't speak. When I hugged him, he cried uncontrollably. Billy and I helped him upstairs to bed and later when the children came home from school they peeped in on him as he slept. Shirley, our neighbour, who had waited with me during those terrible hours of not knowing, brought in a tray of tea and we sat at the bottom of the stairs in relieved silence.

Our Venture eventually made the journey to Holyhead the following May and I stood at the end of McKenzie jetty as she was towed onto her new mooring in the harbour. The seas were flat calm with hardly a breath of wind as she slipped past the breakwater and into her new home.

Robert towed her by lifeboat, assisted by his friend Roy Meakin. She was to carry him out on other sea journeys over the next few years but he would never doubt her seaworthiness after surviving the hurricane of 1976.

Fishermen from as far away as the Hebrides telephoned our home to speak to Robert for they recognised the miracle of survival in that terrible storm. Robert changed forever. His youth and strength diminished for he had given himself to the sea. For months he lost the fear of death, which was terrifying in itself to me. He rarely talks about that ill-fated voyage but remains convinced that when the moon lit up those raging seas for those few minutes, he was given back his life.

In Roger Dunn's house, in Par Cornwall, sits the Bible that was the only thing that remained in the cabin when all else was washed away. Each man had saved the other's life and each man was left to dream and ponder on the great force that had changed their lives forever.

HOLYHEAD BREAKWATER

Working the Boat

OUR VENTURE.
Our Venture moored at McKenzie Jetty

Our Venture worked the seas between Holyhead and the Skerries, conveying dedicated fishermen from Birmingham, Manchester and even as far as Plymouth to float and fish hundreds of feet above the many wrecks; each of which marked the horrors of the Irish Sea, which rose beyond challenge of the finest navigators.

The Irish Sea. I spent many evenings walking along McKenzie jetty and gazing out beyond the breakwater for the first glimpse of the blue bow of *Our Venture* bringing home the man I shared my life and dreams with.

Sometimes the seas would boil and even at the end of the jetty, I would feel unsafe. On summer evenings my thin cotton dress would flap and cling to me and I would involuntarily place my hands across my empty womb, protecting a nest from which the baby had been taken long ago. Fat and sturdy, he was now tucked up in his cot, or imaginatively cared for by his two sisters.

On these nights, as I stood waiting for the boat to come in, I would wonder about all our futures, including the young man who was entertaining the paying fishermen with sea stories and adventures so varied that even with a poor catch, they poured ashore red faced and joking, united in their journey. Once again they were ready to find their land legs and face yet again their city homes.

Bookings for the next trip would be made there and then on the jetty and I would watch them lugging their catch up the steps, smelling of sea spray and fish and I'd smile at their rediscovery of sea journeys, which are part of so many men's blood.

Then I would lean over the cold rail and watch the slim young man as he washed down the decks, checked the equipment, started up the engine and motored out to the mooring. On rough days he would grapple and catch the buoy in three attempts.

On a calm day he moored in one single stretch of the boat hook. On sunny days he often swam out to the mooring.

The dinghy would be rowed to shore and dragged up onto a little shelf, which the children had named 'Stoney Beach'. Here there were the old wooden remnants of an old lifeboat ramp, which was only a few minutes walk from our small cottage.

It was a routine almost as old as time in Holyhead. Like so much in this area it was his life and I was just an observer.

The Skerries

On a fine day, if you look out over the Irish Sea from Holyhead, you can see a small group of islands known as the Skerries. For many years they have housed a manned lighthouse to warn shipping of the treacherous rocks. But their place in the history of the area goes much further. It is this history that forms part of the character of the people of this corner of Wales.

Long ago the real ruler of Gwynedd made his escape from Anglesey to these islands, fleeing for his life along with his friends. It was then known as the Islands of the Seals.

It happened like this. About ten years before William I conquered England in the Battle of Hastings in 1066, Gruffudd of Cynan was born. Gruffudd, King of Gwynedd, was born in Ireland in the city of Dublin. His father was Cynan, King of Gwynedd, and his mother was Ragnhildr, daughter of Olaf, King of the city of Dublin. Gruffudd was of noble birth and royal race and although his father died when he was quite young, his mother Ragnhildr always told her son that he was the rightful King of Gwynedd. Gruffudd waited for the day when he could take an army to Wales and seize his land.

When he was twenty years old, he gathered together many Irish men and Danes who would help him and sailed in ships to Wales. His mother was a Dane and therefore he included that race of people. Gathering more supporters as he crossed Wales, Gruffudd fought battles on the Welsh mainland. He returned to his palace on Anglesey to discover that his army was quarrelling. The Welsh disliked both Irish and Danes and finally there was a rebellion. Only the men of Anglesey and part of Caernarvonshire helped Gruffudd. There was a great battle in which he rode his horse and used his double-edged sword. His friends feared for his life and a nobleman from Anglesey caught the bridle of his horse and dragged him from the battle. They escaped on a small boat, which carried them to rocky islands called the Islands of the Seals. Then they returned to Ireland.

In one year Gruffudd had won a Kingdom and lost it and it would be many years before he eventually returned as ruler, living to an old age. His body is buried in Bangor Cathedral to the left of the high altar.

For a number of years I had stared out from the mainland and wondered about the Skerries. What fears and hopes did Gruffudd carry with him as he fled away from his Kingdom? The treacherous currents, which swirled about the small islands, had not smashed his boat. Under cover of darkness he had stolen across the Irish Sea, which had blessed him with his life.

The Light Keeper

The Skerries became closer to me when Robert was asked to sail to the lighthouse with provisions. A treacherous journey, even on calm days, that threatened the bravest navigator because of the tiderips and the narrow entrance that lay to the western side. Once you sailed through, you had to turn hard to starboard to avoid the facing rocks. On calm days it was a difficult manoeuvre, but when the wind has northerly it was impossible to navigate.

There were two light keepers stationed on the largest island, occupied with cleaning the glass of the great light, maintaining the diesel engines that drove it, curtaining the great beam in the morning and generally maintaining the light house, thus protecting shipping from Ireland, Scotland, Liverpool and The Isle of Man.

Many lighthouses were automatic, but when we lived in Holyhead, the Skerry lighthouse was manned. Two men worked a month on and a month off. Trinity House supplied the diesel and fresh water but required Robert to exchange light keepers and take out engineers if anything went wrong.

Robert described to me the ground nesting birds, rabbits and big seals that basked on the rocks. Scattered all over the islands were tiny rock floors and thin fragile grass. It was a miniature paradise inaccessible to man. When the herring gulls laid their first eggs on the ground, the light keepers would mark some of them with a cross. When the second eggs were laid, they took them for food. Occasionally Robert would bring home a dozen of these eggs and make a huge omelette combined with onions. The light keepers would lay lobster pots around the rocks and feast on occasional lobsters and crabs.

On foggy days or nights the huge foghorn would send its chilly deep voice across the sea, and during those times the light keepers had very little sleep. I used to wonder what kind of men would live in such isolation and was always relieved to see Our Venture returning to Holyhead after a visit to this lonely place.

One day Robert received a call concerning one of the light keepers. He had a fish bone stuck in his throat and needed to be brought ashore as soon as possible. Robert informed the light-keeper by radio that the weather was poor and that he must be prepared to jump aboard Our Venture, as he would be unable to tie up owing to the bad weather.

My opportunity to visit the Skerries had arrived and I begged Robert to take me with him. He hesitated, looking up at the dark sky, but I insisted. Climbing aboard, we set off through rising seas. As we left the end of the breakwater, spray hit the bow and Robert shook his head grimly. Urged on by the thought of the light keeper choking to death, we ploughed deeper through heavier seas.

Then we were in a no man's land, Holyhead shrinking to a blur and the Skerries not even visible. There was no turning back now and I felt rising fear, which silenced any questions.

Through the windstorm we could see the tops of smashing seas, breaking over jagged rocks when Robert suddenly turned and grinned. Did I know that the light keeper was twenty-five stone and that his girlfriend was the fat lady in a sideshow at a circus?

I looked up amazed for I had screwed up my eyes tightly during the last thirty minutes of that hellish journey. Had Robert gone mad? What bizarre information was he feeding to me? I laughed hysterically but my voice was swept away in the howling wind and my young man stood resolute at the wheel, concentrating on the great feat that lay ahead. Like a jagged mouth, the entrance to the Skerries leered at us, beckoning us to throw the dice. Without hesitation, the little trawler surged forward like an arrow, high on a green swell. I could touch the rocks on either side, as she shot through on a high sea, into the restless lagoon.

Robert swung around to face the entrance and manoeuvred towards the rocks; twenty ton of oak pressed into a boat as round as an apple. The Deutsche engine throbbed consistently and I opened my eyes to see a twenty-five stone light keeper balanced on the rocky shore! Amazed, I saw him spring and leap forwards, landing with a very heavy thud on the fore deck. Cleverly, he'd waited until Our Venture came up on the rise of a swell so that his leap to freedom was successful. Staggering and clutching his throat he stumbled into the wheelhouse where I was crouched.

Robert steamed full ahead for the entrance and when I opened my eyes again the Skerries were behind us, splintering the green seas with their jagged rocks. By this time a huge swell was running. Water black and treacherous was thundering past each side of the boat and solid walls of water rolled and broke over the bow. I was terrified! My heart thumping, I crouched down in the wheelhouse and prayed for our safety.

Then I turned my attention to the huge man who lay across me, his head in my lap. He was sweating profusely and had turned nasty reddish purple. Taking off my jacket, I wiped his face with it and comforted him in my arms. I stroked his big head but dared not move my trapped legs from beneath his seemingly dying body. We both began to vomit, loudly and repeatedly into the local supermarket plastic bags, each one of which I knotted when it was full!

The noise of the sea was thunderous and we had to shout at each other during that dreadful journey. In desperation I talked about everything that came into my mind in order to keep him conscious; poetry, friendship, love, children, on and on until we lay there together, totally exhausted.

Meanwhile, Robert reached the harbour and McKenzie jetty where an ambulance was waiting. Miraculously my poor light keeper lurched to his feet and heavily assisted, he staggered up the jetty steps and into the ambulance.

I returned home and slept for twenty-four hours, vowing never to go to sea again. When I phoned the hospital to enquire about the light keeper, I discovered that the fishbone had been dislodged from his throat during the vomiting! The following week I was shown a lyrical Welsh letter printed in the local paper written "To Janice," praising my rescue and nursing. There was little mention of the skipper!

Soon after though, and despite my horrifying one-and-only experience of the Skerries in close up, I found myself looking out there again, thinking of Gruffudd, and realised the magic of Wales was again at work on my soul.

THE SKERRIES LIGHTHOUSE

The Cannon

Lying on the bed of the sea off North Stack is a cannon that was originally used to warn shipping before the foghorn was introduced. During the year of the Queen's Jubilee in 1977 the Sea Cadets from London set out to retrieve the cannon, which lay at the foot of the cliffs where it had been pushed once it was redundant. Making an enormous effort, they managed to ease it off the rocks with pulleys at low tide. A frame of forty-five gallon drums would float it into Holyhead at high tide.

During the week, a number of small fishing boats failed to tow in the cannon and finally the sea cadets asked Robert if he could use Our Venture for the rescue. Our entire family went aboard the trawler that day to rescue the cannon, quite forgetting my vow that I'd never go aboard again after the Skerries rescue. The weather was calm but a bad gale was forecast. The cannon had to be pulled around North Stack before the seven-knot tide turned, for it was impossible to steam against such a tide.

Quickly we boarded our boat, feeling quite safe, as the gale was not expected for several hours. The heavy rope was attached to the frame of the cradle in which rested the cannon and we began to pull the huge dead weight. Triumphantly we neared the end of North Stack but Our Venture slowed down as the tide turned and we began to be dragged backwards. We were too late, the tide had beaten us. We tied the cannon onto the rocks back at North Stack, but that night the gale broke it free, making it a danger to shipping and so the sea cadets made the decision to sink it. A marksman with 303 rifle shot holes into the forty-five gallon drums and their prize trophy slipped to the rocky depths.

For a long time they said it was irretrievable and certainly as long as we remained in Holyhead, it rested deep beneath the waves. But someone who has lived in this part of the world for a time never really leaves it and I talk from time to time with old friends and was amused to think that even though Holyhead remains always the same in my mind, that things do change; I recently heard that the cannon was finally raised and now stands mounted outside the lifeboat station in Trearddur Bay.

Death

One of my closest friends drowned out there, somewhere beyond the breakwater. His boat was lost with all hands. The sea, a great lover, took him in her arms and claimed him forever. Distraught people, who loved him so much, make up stories about this fisherman. They said he never drowned at all, he ran away, and now lives now in Ireland just a few hours across the sea, but I know in my heart that he is clutched to the icy bosom of those cold waters.

On calm days we always knew the capricious nature of the tides and sudden weather changes. We all, who linked our lives to that sea, knew the risks. But we all still ventured out there. And we all still grieved terribly when the sea took its right and claimed one of us. Perhaps the stories about miraculous escape to a new life were the way they all coped with death and allowed them to live peacefully with such a treacherous neighbour.

SOUTH STACK, HOLYHEAD

Look at me when I'm talking to you Billy!

On many occasions a number of fishing boats would moor at McKenzie jetty for parties of fisherman to disembark. Robert would work through the night, wash down the decks and leave within the hour with another fishing trip. In between those times, the jetty became a meeting place of boats with much clambering onto fishing vessels where an exchange of information, joking and laughing occurred. I would rush down to the jetty at dawn to supply Robert with provisions and details of the next coach arrival.

Half dressed, and half asleep, I would walk down to the boats, lean on the rails high above Our Venture and watch the lively exchanges below. I never boarded the boat but occasionally I would shout out messages to Robert or wave to someone I knew. One summer day I saw Billy Edwards on board Our Venture and both he and Robert were laughing together as they sat on the door of the fish hold.

I yelled down at them but neither took any notice. Feeling irritable, I yelled again and Billy looked up at me, directly above him. He turned away very quickly and faced Robert. "Look at me when I'm talking to you Billy," I screamed out, but still there was no reaction and both men began to chuckle to themselves. Feeling annoyed by their childish behaviour I returned home, pushing the incident from my mind as I busied myself with my routine of work and managing a household of three boisterous children.

Several weeks later, I was fast asleep in bed one night when I was awakened by loud laughter. Creeping down the stairs, I stood behind the kitchen door, identifying Robert's friends, who had returned for drinks after the pub. Their conspiratorial whispers confirmed my suspicions and I leaned against the door to catch what they were saying. Then I had a shock. In his lilting Welsh voice I heard Billy mimic me. "Look at me when I'm talking to you Billy!" He repeated this again and again, followed by more whispering and deeper laughter.

Puzzled, I returned to bed but couldn't dismiss the incident from my mind. I was fuming, then upset at the thought that a man I so liked could be so cruel about me – and at Robert for not defending me. The following morning I could wait no longer and challenged Robert. His reaction wasn't what I was expecting. Hanging his head and looking distinctively embarrassed, he confessed to me that when I'd stood on the jetty that day, I hadn't been wearing any knickers!

My shock and anger soon turned to laughter when I thought about Billy, so gentlemanly and quite shy, being placed in such a position, in every way! The lesson was learned about making sure I was properly awake before heading down to the jetty though. Over the years, a number of visitors to our home have been mystified when they have heard either Robert or I sing out those words and both burst out laughing!

ADMIRALTY PIER, HOLYHEAD

Other Travellers

Others have journeyed to Holyhead, some almost accidentally as though escaping from dark shadows on the mainland. They ran away from England towards the distant Welsh Mountains, past the ancient castles of Conway and Caernarfon, and then turned towards the sea. They sought another life in another country.

Holyhead has many English residents who were initially charmed by holidays on Anglesey and returned for the remainder of their lives, shunning their English heritage.

It remains a lure, enticing men over the Menai Bridge, which spans the treacherous Menai Straits. They travel across to the island far from the mountains of the mainland, as many others have before them.

They cross an ancient island, one established for tourists and a deeper, more complex one sustained by the Welsh, their ancestors guiding their ultimate decisions. Still further they journeyed, crossing onto Holy Island, innocent of its complexities.

Here the Druids once practiced their pagan rituals. Despite a Roman invasion and massacre of these pagans, the mist that often rolled over from the Irish Sea shrouding Holyhead Mountain and both islands, evokes a sense of history.

There is seriousness about Anglesey. It is not a place to be taken lightly.

Holyhead has cast its spell on you and you are never free of it.

Rest Well Anglesey

Rest well Anglesey, and all the dear people within you, both past and present. You will remain long after I am gone, a Welsh island thickly steeped in history, language and memories. Others will come to your shores and without knowing why, they will feel the breath of history upon them and sense that this is a place worth fighting for. Without even opening a history book, like Gruffudd of Cynan nine hundred years ago, they will make their own mark on this mysterious place.

Working in a Welsh Secondary school was a unique experience and one that was to play an important part in my future life. I was one of very few non Welsh speaking teachers amongst a staff who were fluent in their first language, having been educated in North Wales where Welsh is proudly spoken.

Quite often I found myself sitting in a school assembly, listening to a strange language. A short distance away in the Primary school my children were learning Welsh as a second language. Of course, I couldn't know how this experience would resonate for me years later in other schools, in other places and with other languages.

I slowly began to appreciate why the Gaelic tongue held the key to the survival of the Welsh culture.

I came to realise that everyone who has lived there has written their own history, through their individual and community experiences.

Their stories may not be of kings and great armies, but they become part of the folklore of Holyhead. Small and precious, their retelling is an invaluable part of the charm and allure of Holy Island.

ST SEIRIOL'S CHURCH, HOLYHEAD

Chapter Seven:

Going South 1980 - 1987

Cornwall

We seemed so happy and settled in Holyhead. So it was a shock when Robert announced one day that he would like to take *Our Venture* to Cornwall and work with Roger Dunn. My immediate reaction was a negative one as I remembered that terrible sea journey of several years earlier, but Robert reassured me that once we had sold our house, he would arrange for a tow behind a coaster that was sailing to Cornwall. A good friend of mine at the school bought our house and before the completion date the tow was organised. Robert would leave at midnight and the sea journey would hopefully be free of complications. I felt very anxious as the wind began to blow that afternoon and the weather forecast wasn't good.

Robert packed the boat with provisions and cheerfully set off. By midnight I had begun to feel more relaxed and finally went off to bed. I was awakened by Robert standing in the doorway of the bedroom looking very shaken. His arms were covered with oil and he looked totally dejected. He had set off behind the coaster but when she reached North Stack she was motoring far too fast. Water started to pour in through the rudderpost and sadly Robert had to admit defeat and let go of the ropes. He turned *Our Venture* and motored home. At that point he most probably revisited the trauma of the terrible sea journey with Roger, and encouraged by me he decided that his boat didn't want to leave Welsh waters. She had after all served her ultimate purpose in saving two men's lives and he decided not to push her into any more long journeys.

We put her up for sale and as we were leaving within days for Cornwall, he asked his friend Glyn Shergo to look after the sale of the boat. Fortunately she sold quickly and we heard later that she was fishing out of Bangor.

The children and I headed for Cornwall in appalling weather. The floods were so atrocious that farmers were checking on their sheep by canoe! Robert drove the removal van down and within days we had occupied a very dilapidated, but potentially fine house that overlooked the beach at Par. More importantly, it was situated only a few doors away from Roger Dunn's home.

As Robert no longer owned a boat he turned his hand to building, and I won a position as a Drama teacher at the local secondary school at Fowey. We spent six happy years in Cornwall, although Robert longed for his boat and missed fishing. At times he would help Roger on one of his trawlers but Our Venture was never far from his mind. The boatman's job with Roger never materialised, which saddened Robert. He had always told me that the Cornish fiercely guarded their employment as there is so little of it available in Cornwall and Roger could not fly in the face of the wind and risk the disapproval of his fellow workers, and so the potential job never materialised.

Once again Robert took to fishing the lakes and rivers of Cornwall. Much to my amusement he began to invent weird concoctions that he called 'boilies'. These resembled soft round pink sweets that were brightly coloured. He never revealed the ingredients of these strange objects but assured me that they would entice any fish into taking the bait even if impaled on a sharp little hook! The children, intrigued by the 'sweeties', sampled several of them but declared that they were quite disgusting so Robert's invention was quite safe. Stored in the fridge in multiple numbers, they became the subject of much conversation over dinner when we had all returned from school and Robert from his fishing trips.

I began to hear of the deep silent pools hidden from the roadside by thick woods, Robert ventured further afield to discover several man made lakes. He finally met a fellow fisherman who was also after the elusive giant carp, which bubbled away in the deep mud, only rising to the surface on hot humid days. Sometimes I would accompany Robert at the weekends, but we never met his fishing friend.

Meanwhile, I continued to work in a school whose culture was so much more relaxed than my Welsh teaching experience. The children came from a wide variety of backgrounds including farms, fishing villages, and the frequent newcomers from London and the southern counties. The beauty of Cornwall beckoned and town and city houses were exchanged for the picture postcard beauty of the south west of England.

The headmaster of the school was pleasant but quite remote, anxious to promote a high quality of education in the pupils and I was never really able to relate to him on any matter. Once he realised that a member of his staff was caring, efficient and put the pupils first, work was not interrupted by heavy management. So the school days passed pleasantly enough and at one point my two children attended the school.

One summer evening I decided that I would go with Robert on one of his fishing expeditions to the man made lakes. As we climbed the hill, we could see the lakes in the distance through the hazy late evening sun. I spotted a fisherman on the other side of the water, a solitary figure surrounding by all his fishing gear.

Robert smiled with approval. "There's my friend. You can meet him at last."

"What's his name?"

Robert laughed. "I've never asked him his name, we're too busy tricking the carp!" As we approached, Robert called out, "Caught any mate?" and his friend looked up. It was the headmaster of the school where I taught!

Our years spent in Cornwall are now a distant memory of tiny fishing villages, Roger's Cornish laugh, my children growing up into those difficult adolescent years, satisfying times spent teaching and lanes and hedges spilling over with spring flowers. I was never to anticipate at this time in my life that I would face the next seventeen years working in the most traumatic and challenging environment of all, yet looking back over my teaching career I can see how well it prepared me for the most fulfilling experiences in my life.

Chapter Eight:

South Australia 1987 - 2005

Emigrant

There are days
when ships have a silence
the seas an emptiness
when decks of faces
stare at feint horizons
trace the edges of vast oceans,
mutter words from homesick songs
full of bleak emotions,
and when there's no going back
the doldrums slowly pass
and they talk of promised lands
a mapping out of empires
of chipping in to make fortunes

They barter bed linen, swap hands,
gamble investments, trade rings
as the boat navigates the shifting sands
and docks by the tempting lagoon.
Land-locked from home
some turn their heads towards the sea
and look into infinity
while others, seem to come alive
with possibilities and make to the City
with a revived sense of energy

So as the boat turns its back for another voyage
it splits the pack, and spews them out
to go their different ways
They haul their bags down the line;
greys dissolving into mercurial gold
and all the deals are off.

Ryan Ó Conaill

Look up at the Stars

There have been many occasions when a line of shoes both big and small have been left on my front doorstep, my visitors being entire families who brought into my home their cares and concerns of settlement in their new country. Often with one of their children as interpreter, they endeavoured to resolve problems or simply turned up to share a special occasion through prepared food, old photographs and smiles.

One day I received a very ornate wedding invitation through the post. It was from one of my students almost a decade ago. I was invited to his wedding and as I prepared to go I thought back to the time when I first knew this particular Cambodian boy. My initial work with him involved dealing with the horrific trauma, which haunted him from his early life when he and his parents escaped from the Khmer Rouge soldiers during the Pol Pot days of Cambodia.

He told me repeatedly about his childhood in a village north of Phnom Penh, which became a place of unspeakable terror during the war. His family hid in the forest, living on vegetation, rats, monkeys, plants and even soil.

His mother was heavily pregnant and as the soldiers drew near the family had to run. His mother fell as she was carrying him in her arms and the burden was too great. As they lay in the fields in the protective darkness, she gave birth to her child and both of them died. The young boy scraped a hole under a bamboo bush and buried them before following his father to a refugee camp over the border in Thailand.

Many more dreadful incidents occurred but none as great as leaving his dead mother behind. As he grew older and eventually came to Australia he coped well, keeping hidden the terrible memory, which he thought he'd buried back in that field in Cambodia.

Now our little classroom was the silent witness to the outpourings of grief far beyond tears. His deep mourning, guilt and sadness washed over him in unpredictable waves over the next two years, his greatest wish being to see his mother's photo as he couldn't remember her face. Together we shared these unsolvable wishes until one day he came in, eyes lit up, to announce that he had dreamed of his mother and saw her face smiling at him!

Educational progress was swift then and he became a handsome and independent young man. He visited my home when he had finished school and when I saw him to the gate I dared to ask him how he had coped during that time of spiritual searching. He smiled, a slow sad smile and told me to look upwards into the night sky at a handful of scattered stars.

"When I was running, running to escape, that time in the forest, I used to look up at the stars. When I came to your classes you always told us to believe in ourselves, to look up at the heavens and know there was something greater than us. It made sense to me. Those two thoughts fitted together."

I watched him drive off, a warrior of the twentieth century and I felt very humbled.

On the day of the wedding I was curious when I parked the car some distance from the city restaurant. There were many parked cars. I felt uncomfortable in my plain cotton dress for it occurred to me that this was possibly a very grand wedding.

As I drew nearer I recognized hundreds of Cambodian friends including the monk who attended my evening language classes. At the doorway in a long line, which disappeared inside the building, was the entire extended family of my student, all beautifully dressed in their traditional Cambodian clothes.

I looked inside to see a tall young man in a grey suit, welcoming each person individually in both Khmer and English. I called his name and he turned, greeting me with a huge smile. Walking past his family he gave me a big hug.

The entire restaurant was booked and fitted out with many round tables, each of which seated six people. There was a waitress for every table, which had as its centrepiece superb wines and spirits. The wedding ceremony itself had been carried out in the Cambodian temple in traditional dress that morning. Now was the time for relaxing and enjoyment. Once again I felt very underdressed at such a formal gathering, but it appeared to make no difference as I was shown by my student to a special table on a balcony that ran the length of the restaurant. From it the entire floor ground floor was easily visible.

I stared down at the floor below, wondering how he felt, the young man whom I had known during those sad years. I felt so proud of him that tears welled in my eyes. As I fought my emotions and struggled to smile like all those around me, he came on to the dance floor below me, holding the arm of his bride, and made a speech in English.

He thanked everyone including me. Then he surprised me by raising his glass, with the entire gathering followed suit, and called out an invitation to me. "Please come down and dance the first dance with me."

As I stumbled down the stairs with eyes full of tears, I dimly remembered that I couldn't dance! But it made no difference as my student waltzed me around the floor to clapping. As we danced I was unable to speak and finally as the music came to a close I climbed the stairs again, thankful that such an emotional moment was over.

Then I realised that my left hand was clutching a piece of paper. My student had pushed it into my hand as we whirled around the dance floor. For thirty minutes I held it then when no one was looking, I slowly opened the paper and there in unmistakable handwriting it said "The Starlight Room" and the name of the most expensive hotel in the city! Puzzled, I waited until all the family photographs had been taken, and then I approached my student for an explanation.

"Yes that's right. There is a car to take you there. My present to you is to spend a night close to the stars."

Sure enough I was taken to the most expensive room on the top floor of the hotel and I pulled the curtains open to reveal a sky covered by stars.

That night I never slept. Instead I stayed awake and thought about the humbling experience of working with such students and all that they had taught me. I am grateful for it – and for them, because their lives give meaning to my existence.

Home Visit

Mikhail waited for me in the faculty office while I finished telephoning, writing out a fax and many other little jobs. I was aware of his intensity as he sat watching me; I glanced at him, noting his fine features: half boy, half man, self contained, solitary. I did not understand him.

This was a long awaited time, decided upon by me the previous year when things were not going well. Fights and paybacks and never backing away from confrontation brought him to the attention of the administration. Last week, he had been ordered to remove his jacket, which was not school uniform, and he did so during a heavy storm, thus becoming soaked, yet he appeared indifferent, almost matter of fact regarding his punishment.

That last week when I noticed his soaked clothing I asked him again about the home visit and suddenly it was arranged. His mother would be in and would receive me. We drove home, searching for conversation. I talked about my old VW Beetle and its history but he remained silent apart from verbal instructions that led us through a public housing estate.

Then his voice changed. "There's my house." And we pulled into the drive of an Australian bungalow with a lovely garden. Newly planted rose bushes cared for and nurtured lined the path. Mikhail smiled a slow warm smile, relaxing as he climbed from the car, carefully lifting his bag from the floor. I realised then that he was proud to bring me home. His father, dark, handsome and bearded, was waiting in the drive and he beckoned me to drive under the carport, pointing at the sun.

I smiled but no words were said between us. I reached out and shook his hand. He and Mikhail spoke in Russian, and then I was inside the gloom of the house, blinking after the bright sunshine outside. The living room was small and neat, and on a dining table lay the Malaccan Bibles, three large holy books, well thumbed through and opened to appropriate pages. I quickly glanced around the room noting that all the reading matter was in Russian; even the videos had Russian titles.

And then Mikhail's mother came in, welcoming me to her family home. In contrast to her husband she was very pale and worn. Her lovely smile welcomed me as we sat in the small room opposite each other, both from Europe, both carrying the burden and anxiety of motherhood. Why had I come here I asked myself. What was I searching for? I smiled again and all three watched me carefully.

I began to ask about Armenia. Had they seen the recent television program that showed the leaking reactor threatening a nuclear disaster, that could wipe out Europe? Words began to flow. Mother understood English quite well while Mikhail confidently and appropriately interpreted for his father. I was aware of the total respect and love between them, an understanding born of love, tolerance and sharing. Whatever had troubled Mikhail had not been nurtured in this environment.

And so began their poignant and moving story of life in Armenia, one of great poverty and suffering. First came the great earthquakes of 1988 which shook Armenian soil at precisely 11.40am on the 7th of December. Mikhail was eight years old at the time and he told me of the disaster, eyes wide, reliving a monstrous event which according to the Malaccans, only God could have created.

Leninakan (now Gyumri), a city of thousands was terribly damaged and Kirovakan (now Vanadzan), and Spitak were flattened, houses disappearing forever, swallowed up into the bowels of an angry earth. Armenians in the capital of Yerevan, including Mikhail's family, went to the assistance of those who had been spared. Mikhail described the legless, headless mass of mutilated bodies, the screaming and the silence, the great cracks in the walls and the chasms into which people fell. In the small villages many wondered at the many Malaccans who did not die as all around them perished.

Mikhail's mother sighed, raising her hands in disbelief as her husband and son described those scenes. Reassured by each other, they had been in wonderment at the human suffering.

Mikhail talked of 1993, when he only knew twenty minutes of electricity in each twenty-four hours, supplied by the leaking nuclear power stations. On the ninth floor of the concrete flats, he and his eight brothers and sisters lived out their lives around their family, while his father visited Moscow many times, flying there at great expense to approach the Australian Embassy. Their eldest son had already left for Australia but they would eventually become poverty stricken in their efforts to join him.

Mikhail's father's family, including his mother, brothers and sisters are still all living close to the power station. He phones his mother only to hear her cry for her lost son, lost to Australia. He knows he will never see her again. I referred again to the power station and was informed that it has now been reopened and declared safe, although still leaking. People are forced to harness its evil power so that they can have energy for light and cooking.

"Ah," they said. "It is a beautiful land, our Armenia. There are great rivers and mountains and big forests. The wild berries taste so sweet and we pick the fruit of the countryside. "

Mikhail's mother continued. "We are economical – we have to be. We visit each other's homes, we talk, we laugh, we suffer together and we take comfort from our religion. That is life in Armenia."

She went on. "Australia is a wonderful place, yet it is silent. I say, 'good morning, good afternoon, goodnight', and my neighbours do not answer. They say, 'do you cook every day? Why do you cook?' I cook because it is my life as we sit around our table of good home food and give thanks to our God."

Appropriately we all rose, as in a congregation, and I was led forward, escorted by Mikhail, to another room. To my astonishment I saw a table laden with food. Mikhail's mother smiled with pride. She and Mikhail had worked into the night to prepare such delicacies ready for the visit. I felt overwhelmed and fought back my tears. I sat down opposite Mikhail's father and by the side of my student, who by then was my teacher. Strange little dishes of unknown food lay in front of me. Unbuttered white bread was the only thing I recognised. My cup was of the finest china beside a tiny glass bowl to hold the tea bag. Hot water was poured from a huge silver pot. As I took my napkin, Mikhail laid a hand on my arm, restraining me. Gently he explained. We must stand for prayers and prayers would be said again at the end of the meal.

We stood silently and I shut my eyes. I could hear a soft Russian voice and I turned to look. Mikhail was praying in his Malaccan religion. His prayers were long and I needed them for I felt that I couldn't swallow their beautiful food, prepared with such love and care. But we sat and ate, comfortable with each other now that the barrier of the horrors of Armenia had been overcome.

Photos were passed to sand fro. I talked of my own children and of other beloved family. We discussed the real issues of life; shopping, preparing food and cooking. We commented on the searing heat, which tired all of us. We talked of mortgages and lack of cool air and of Mikhail's father's car which he had named 'the old lady' as she was no longer in use, being unfit for the road.

Through he open door I spotted pigeons, many breeds including fantails, which carried me back to England and my father's allotment. He had kept pigeons and since that time I have always longed to. Mikhail noticed that I was looking outdoors and with great pride he informed me that all the pigeons – at least sixty, were his.

Mikhail led me outside and we stood in his dark pigeon shed. I shut my eyes and listened to the soft cooing noise. I loved that noise. We both stood there quietly. Mikhail began checking on the new babies, lifting them lovingly to his face and in my memory I was standing in another shed a long time ago, surrounded by all the paraphernalia that my father hoarded away from my mother's tidying hand.

As we crossed the back yard he pointed to the top of three pine trees. Perched high were his white fantails.

"They are free," he smiled and he suddenly clapped his hands and watched them with narrowed eyes as they soared into the sky.

"Mikhail, it's good that you can keep pigeons now that you're not living in a ninth floor flat."

"Oh, I still kept pigeons in Armenia. I kept them on the roof."

There was nothing I could tell this boy. He had in that house what so many of us have lost – security and beliefs as well as painful memories that continue to be brought into the light and a childhood being lived out in a foreign land. His strength is nurtured by the love of this family as they stand strong and firm together.

I understood Mikhail now.

I realized that he didn't pick fights; he just didn't back away from them. Because he'd had to fight for so much more. And he hadn't cared about getting wet because he had known greater hardship. But most of all that he knew what was important and what wasn't; what was worth being bothered over and what wasn't and that only comes from wisdom beyond the years and security born of being loved and knowing how to love.

The Guinea Pig Girl

I look back with amusement on my initial experience in an Australian school.

It was a hot January day, so hot that I was fascinated by the strength of the sun and people's acceptance of such a climate.

I had endured a forty minute drive out to the northern suburbs of Adelaide and the heat was terrifying me! I allowed memories of the gentle Cornish lanes to surround me, smiling as I recalled the day I pulled up in my VW Beetle on the way to Fowey School one June morning and lay amongst the bluebells on the grass verge.

"I'm not made for this heat," I thought grimly, not considering my unsuitable clothes, stockings and high heeled shoes - every article of clothing for the sun to attack! And it did!

Thus my first day in an Australian school! The Principal welcomed me with a nod of his head, instructing the caretaker to show me to a dusty classroom that had been used for storage, and that was where I remained for that first year.

I was to be the English as a Second Language teacher and within that small room would crouch the horrors of the Cambodian Pol Pot regime and resulting madness, the journeys from Chile, escapes from Vietnam and much more. Writing poured from students at a prolific pace, despite some of them being at school for the first time in their lives.

Explanations flowed, prayers to Buddha were constant, and a year nine Cambodian boy discovered that the world was not flat!

As they made their discoveries, I discovered that I was at the beginning of a long journey towards an understanding of grief, the effects of torture, the joy of family reunion and the worship of education.

Food was brought in, discussed, swapped and shared. I had to decline such delicacies as the uncooked embryos in duck eggs, offered to me by Heng as he tucked into this Cambodian delicacy, crunching tiny beaks, wet, barely formed feathers and bony feet.

One Cambodian student, locked into the room during extreme times of anguish, would smash his head on the wall to relieve the pain of his escape from Phnom Penh to the Thai border. He blamed himself for his mother's death as she tried to escape from the soldiers.

This was my introduction to an Australian school.

And what of the Principal? He was unusual! He strode about the school, unlocking doors, checking classrooms, nodding but not smiling. He knew the names of every student. I had never come across such a person. I didn't understand how he worked or why the place appeared to hum, - that quiet invisible quality that you sense in a peaceful and successful school.

One day as we worked in the small room, we heard shouting and angry voices that travelled from the foyer, bounced off the walls of the corridor and invaded our peace!

We listened. It continued. Annoyed, I marched crossly down the corridor to see the Principal towering over a small unyielding girl who stood before him, shoulders straight in defiance.

He glared at her and pointed at something. Then I heard the words, "You will NOT bring that guinea pig into school ever again!"

Back came the firm reply, "I will! You can't STOP me!"

The Principal seemed to tower in height. Being already over six feet tall, he looked enormous.

"You will NOT bring that guinea pig in ever again! It's run around the science lab with thirty students chasing it, it's chewed up books in the English room, And what is more! (raised voice) it PEES all the time! For goodness sake girl, it's peeing on you right now!"

I glanced down and to my horror I saw little drips of yellow liquid seeping through the girl's skirt and forming a small wee puddle on the floor! I was terrified. She was defiant. The Principal by now was purple in the face and ready for a brain haemorrhage and I hadn't yet sighted the guinea pig!

Now in actual fact I like guinea pigs. Correction, I LOVE guinea pigs - ever since I'd kept two and they'd multiplied to ninety-four all in one year and all at the bottom of my mother's neat garden!

Admittedly they stank and pood in great abundance but there is such joy in a guinea pig, such enthusiasm, and I had spent many adolescent days happily curled up in the guinea pig shed.

Flutters of empathy mingled with memories pushed to the surface. I spoke. "Hrrr Hmmm! Excuse me, can I say something?"

They hadn't seen me standing there. He looked up, red faced and cross. She turned round resentfully and there he was, a huge fat white guinea pig clutched to her breast, his little eyes anxious and scared. He was a pudding of a guinea pig, a fat, warm, fleshed out comfort blanket. I loved him immediately.

Throwing caution to the wind, I stepped forward into the educational boxing ring and challenged authority.

"Don't send her home. Let me take her to our classroom. I will solve the problem."

He glared at her and looked thoughtfully at me. "Done!" he said decisively like a businessman, which of course he was.

This was too one sided. "There IS a trade off. If I do this for two weeks PLUS the guinea pig, you must supply me with a square of carpet for that awful classroom where I spend my days."

The space between them and me became a chasm. He frowned. "$200 – no more. See the caretaker," and turning quickly, he walked away.

The guinea pig girl faced me defiantly.

I smiled reassuringly. "I love guinea pigs. Can I hold him?"

Back we went down the corridor and into two weeks of guinea pig projects, huge paintings of the pig, friendships made with students from other lands and my own recalled childhood. Heng promised not to say that he had eaten similar animals during the Cambodian war, and so the guinea pig girl became part of our world.

And the carpet arrived in all its glory and was duly laid one Friday night after school finished.

As for the guinea pig girl - a sad end I'm afraid. She slept with the guinea pig and one night, sheltering underneath her bedclothes to escape the drunken rages of her mother, she rolled on her little friend and squashed him flat!

The Paper Cranes

The Bosnian war was raging. It sent its ripples across the world, carrying its people far from their homeland; within them the untold horrors they had witnessed and been part of, as they escaped the Final Solution, to seek refuge in another part of the earth.

And so it was that one spring day in 1992 the classroom door of a language centre in South Australia opened and a trail of silent students entered. These were no innocent children, for in their eyes was something far beyond lack of just English language. Big boys aged seventeen sat at desks that were far too small for them and they didn't complain. To the left and to the right were the children of Asia and Russia, Eastern Europe, Ethiopia and South America.

The Serb and Bosnian students remained remote, learning methodically and unemotionally. I couldn't reach them, for their suffering had been too great.

One boy insisted on running around the classroom, bending to pick up imaginary pieces of what? The older boys shook their heads and somehow reassured the class that this was all right and to be ignored. Weeks later, when the boy could talk to me a little, he told me he was picking up the pieces of his father.

Stories began to stumble out from numb minds. Dark hidden parts of the brain buried deep; the sinister horrors of war which day and night continued to rage only a jet flight away.

We wept in the classroom for the suffering that was to continue for months. Survival had wiped everything away; emotions, goodbyes, treasured belongings, memories, grandparents, earth that had been tilled for generations. The human spirit had been numbed and bright light almost extinguished. These young men and women had been forced to the edge of humanity and they knew it.

Long before the media began to print stories of the atrocities committed in the name of religion, revenge and possession, these young people hinted of the darkness, which only comes with hate and madness.

The little boy and his friend had sat side by side at school from the age of five until age of fifteen. Then one day the Muslim boy came into school to be confronted by a sea of hate. Going into the schoolyard, he was met with a hail of stones and a threat of being shot. His friend from childhood told him to go and never return to the school that he loved.

Children sheltered in cellars, living on potatoes and water while in the streets above, whole families disappeared. These young people had embraced the comforts of the twentieth century and within the space of a few months, time turned inwards and back down the dark tunnel they were pushed, into a deep morass of ancient vengeance and cruelty. Ill equipped, vulnerable, they suffered unbelievable degradation of their human soul.

I desperately sought to come to terms with this horror, for my language lessons merely gave them words. I wanted them to heal. They were the lucky ones, a mere handful who had escaped from a place of hell. They needed hope.

Then one day a Vietnamese boy made a blue paper crane, following our reading of Sadako and the Thousand Paper Cranes. He carefully threaded it onto a piece of fishing line and hung it from the ceiling. The next day three more appeared, then more and more! We were caught up with this hope, this fragile idea that we could embrace without religion or a past. We would hang one thousand paper cranes from the ceiling of the classroom, and this might give us hope and peace.

Once the idea gained momentum, there was no stopping us. At every opportunity we would fold all available pieces of paper into paper birds. Yes! We would have one made from newspaper, we would make large and minute cranes, we would let them fly at different levels. Asian crane makers sat next to big Serbian and Bosnian boys; gentle Cambodian girls grouped together with Bosnian and Vietnamese girls.

And so the birds appeared. First thirty, then fifty, then one hundred. We used up our lunch hours and breaks and even time at home. Parents joined in and bags of paper cranes appeared. We laughed with delight as the number went up and despaired when several of them fell from the ceiling.

Conversation began to flow. Friendships were made. The wind blew through the open door and we discovered that the cranes moved gently around. On hot days the ceiling fan had the same effect on them.

There were times in that small classroom as we made the birds when we were completely silent, wrapped in our own thoughts, all immigrants and often homesick.

They appointed two girls to count the birds so that one thousand would hang from the ceiling. One of the girls was Serbian and being tall, she could manage the job easily.

I will always remember the day when the thousand birds finally hung from the ceiling. It was on that day that she cried and told me that she had to return to Belgrade as her visa had run out. She and her mother had been visiting an aunt in Australia when the war broke out. Regardless, she must return and re-apply from within the former Yugoslavia. I never sat anyone else at her desk, placing it carefully to one side of the aisle.

The weeks passed by. The students sat proudly under the paper cranes, united in one creative act, which did so much to mend their spirits. We thought of Sadako and how proud she would have been.

Finally came the day of their graduation. At the party we celebrated their success and said our goodbyes. I walked back across the schoolyard. Then I rubbed my eyes in disbelief. For there was the Serbian girl walking, and now running towards me. She threw her arms about me.

Yes, she had her visa, but not before being caught up in the horror of war. She had visited the bombed out ruins of her former home and as she waited for her visa in Belgrade, where she had never been before the war, life had been precarious and dangerous.

But all that came out in a rush. She really wanted something else. Please would I take her to the classroom. She had to look at something.

I pushed open the door and she silently stared at the birds. I pointed out her desk and she sat down. Finally I broke the silence for I desperately needed to know what had given her the faith and strength to survive.

Had she turned to God, prayed for safety?

She turned and smiled. "I thought of our thousand paper cranes and I knew that we would be safe. I have waited all this time to come back and sit beneath them."

In that moment we were united by that single belief, a hope for the human spirit, which can lift itself up and beyond the agony of despair.

We laughed and danced around the room together in relief, then we climbed on top of the desks and I showed her the name of the students written inside the wings of the cranes, including her own.

Chapter Nine:

Seeds of Africa 2005 - Present

Manhunt

(The Sudan genocide 2004/05)

After the chase
stand on the edge
wait for the men
who deliver the wrath of God
You were close enough
to see madness in their eyes
and ran as swift as a gazelle,
the demented dogs
giving you no other direction to go
though should you topple
they will skin you head to toe

Listen to volleys of gunfire
stampede across the empty lake
thundering like herds of wildebeest
great plumes of dust rise like locusts
and vultures trace circles
over hot terracotta stones
picking at the ivory of dead men's bones.

Wait for the great hunters
to stalk for ivory tusks
trophies harvested from the reserve,
easy game stripped and fucked
without a way to run
and silenced by the gun.

Ryan Ó Conaill

The Lost Boys

As a child growing up in England in the 1940s my awareness of Africa was very limited. I imagined it as one country, my imagination fed by the many American films of Tarzan, 'the man of the jungle'.

I can remember coming out of the Saturday cinema session that used to take place at the Odeon in Crewe. Our heads were crammed with the mysterious country of Africa where our hero Tarzan lived, a white man who survived in the jungle, defender of good and protector of animals that understood his language.

Later when we played over the Mill fields the films were recalled in various ways. Boys would imitate the jungle hero, swinging on knotted ropes across the Mill stream.

"Tarzan!" they would scream out as they let go of the rope on the opposite bank, each one imagining the dangers and thrills of the jungle shown in the films.

I pictured Africa as a place of extremes. There was impenetrable jungle and running water that culminated in crashing waterfalls and rapids. Hidden in the tropical undergrowth were gold mines and ancient temples. Animals abounded. Lions padded along well made tracks trodden down by fierce natives. Crocodiles lurked at the muddy water's edge where they invariably ate up the 'baddies'. Usually these characters were avaricious game hunters and safaris of white men who carried ancient maps stolen from the archives of a London museum. They would indicate vast amounts of treasure that could only be retrieved by facing death at least every five minutes.

Natives who were friends with Tarzan would be on one side of the raging river, but cannibals lived on the far bank. From huge distances they would hurl their poisoned spears at white explorers who successfully escaped along the raging rivers, shooting rapids without ever losing their safari hats once, and finally rescuing the immaculately groomed heroine in the story. But she would always be in love with Tarzan and longed to live in his jungle home.

Later we heard about conservation and ivory poaching. But it all seemed so remote. I did once make an actual attempt to reach Africa. I applied for a teaching post in Nairobi during 1962. I was given the position and planned to travel out with a family. They were returning to a property a few miles out from the city.

I informed my family who were very concerned as the Mau Mau terrorists were killing many people at that time. Stubbornly I refused to listen.

My papers were sorted out and I actually had a leaving date.

One morning I came downstairs, drew back the curtains and gazed in horror at a bloodied mess lying on the paving stones of the patio. A ritual circle had been drawn in blood and entrails and chicken feathers had been arranged in the centre including the head of the bird.

I ran screaming to my father who looked very calmly at me.

"When you go expect something like that. Of course it might not be chicken feathers. It is more likely to be you".

The outcome of course was a decision to stay in England. We laughed about it years later but that morning the reality of what was happening a world away hit me.

Slowly the world was alerted to the great famines, which swept across Africa. Television brought hideous footage into every family room. Starving children were held up to the camera; stick like with bulging eyes and distended bellies, these dying babies were held in the arms of skeletal mothers.

It was too huge and complicated a picture for the western world to comprehend. Bob Geldolf's pop concert for aid for Africa in 1985 raised millions of dollars and we sighed with relief. Our consciences were eased by the knowledge that at least aid was going somewhere into that vast continent.

Crisis over, many thought. Then we were shown evidence that all the donations we had raised was not enough. Neither was it hitting the right spots. Some of it was disappearing into the aid agencies themselves, giving concern to the people who had generously contributed their money. Africa became a bit of a memory again and many people thought that the worst of the problems were solved.

As Nelson Mandela had led South Africa from apartheid to multiethnic rule in the 1994 election we had celebrated. Our collective spirits were raised. Once again we could forget Africa. All seemed to be going well there. We had been lulled into a false sense of security as the Cold War came to an end in 1990 and a world of peace and prosperity appeared to be possible.

But great shadows crossed this troubled continent. The ancient enemies within were stirring. Peace broke down in Algeria and Angola. In Somalia a famine raged and order broke down. Civil wars in Sudan, Liberia and Burundi continued.

In 1994 a genocidal rage broke out in Rwanda and once again through television and newspapers we saw the sickening evidence, too great to comprehend, of a county turning on itself. We were unprepared for the savagery of the massacres, but were warned of 'graphic images'. People reached for the remote control. With a flick of a button the images had disappeared and with them our social conscience.

But the random slaughter continued. Reports of Western aid feeding the rebels and stolen food used for buying weapons hardened people's hearts.
One million Hutus moved to Zaire. Amongst them were the rebels, who could not be identified. The United Nations endeavoured to feed the mass and inevitably fed the rebels. The rest of the world was sickened by the savagery of the killings and the mutilation of the bodies.

"Why? Why?" people asked.

Psychologically we began to pull away form this unfathomable disaster. We began to see Africa as a lost cause.

Yet at this very time I can remember walking into a travel agency in Adelaide South Australia and looking in amazement at the glossy travel brochures advertising exotic holidays in tree top reserves in Kenya. All of Africa was not at war but it seemed that way to me.

My understanding of Africa had changed so much from when Tarzan was 'the lost boy'. I thought I knew so much more and laughed at myself when I thought about how naïve I had been as a child and how much I knew now. Life, as always, was about to deal me another lesson.

Unknown to me, a mighty tide of hope arising from terrible suffering was washing towards me. I did not know it. I could never even suspect it. In my lifetime I could never imagine that I could become part of Africa's conscience.

But the gods thought otherwise. They laid the suffering of these people in front of me here in South Australia in 2004 and even then I was unsuspecting. It arrived in innocent ways. A college door opened on 10 Sudanese young men and women one May day in 2004. I was greeted by bright smiles and welcomed.

I agreed to do only a couple of days' teaching each week as I was completing a novel that was preoccupying me and taking up much of my time. How soon that decision would change.

The smiling, welcoming faces belonged to refugees from Sudan, which I identified on a map. I knew very little about it but I relished the thought of teaching English to the adult students. I set about to do good works with the handful of black Africans who had miraculously been plucked from a bloody nightmare that could only be compared with the Holocaust. I ignored the warning signs.

I started my lesson. "Today we will think about sensible diets. Do not eat too many chips or salt. Do not get sucked in to a western diet."

They sat in front of me in the classroom smiling gently and kindly. The average age of the class about twenty-two years. The young men were well over six feet tall and the women were long limbed, tall and elegant. They didn't say anything, just continued to smile.

I pushed further. Food was always a good starting point and a quick way to break the ice. In years of teaching former refugees, it had always been a successful way to start with a class. So I continued.

"Start eating a sensible diet. This means that it must be balanced."

I wrote up the new word on the white board and they repeated it.

Silence in the room. No response, but extreme politeness so I smiled brightly and continued.

"Eating breakfast early in the morning is a sensible way to begin the day."

Makech raised his hand. "Janice, in the camp we eat at night. If we eat in the mornings we can be seen from the air standing in a big group. Perfect for a bombing target. And Janice, we had one meal a day if we were lucky." He cupped his hand to show the amount of food and I sat down feeling ashamed and sickened.

So began my education on the real story of the vast continent of Africa and its complex issues. All around me were refugees. Everyone had a story to tell. Everyone had suffered unimaginably.

I left the college at the end of each day and drove to a local park. Here I sat under the trees and cried. I cried for them and the human race. I cried for myself, frustrated by my stupidity.

The days went by. Now I sat on top of a desk amongst them. I listened carefully to their stories, these beautiful young men and women who have been plucked from their homeland and given a life.

This new life came at a huge cost. They left behind their horrific memories of the longest civil war ever; they left the massive humanitarian disaster that was taking place in the Sudan. They left behind their farming land, bare with famine and defiled by fighting. They left behind a country of forty million people, and the size of Western Australia.

They are part of the continued human tragedy of two million people who have fled their homes.

Many of them were torn from their parents. They left behind their traditional customs and their village life. And worst of all they left behind the memory of thousands of faces, their friends and extended families who remained in the sprawling refugee camps on the Kenyan border. Their guilt and homesickness travelled with them.

Now they questioned their Christian God.

"Why me? What will happen to my people who are left behind at the mercy of diseases such as AIDS and malaria, indiscriminate attacks from tribal people who infiltrate the perimeters of the camp at night and Arab militia who rape, murder and steal from them? What will happen to my people?"

They carry the deeper guilt of survival stories that will never be told. They remember the running from their villages and the separation from their parents during an Arab raid. They heard the cry of babies thrown into the bush as they grew too heavy to carry. Behind them came the thundering of horses and the screams of the dying.

They talked of days crossing deserts with nothing to eat but leaves, earth and lily pads. They found dead lizards to cut up and eat but they are too starved to hunt for food. Some had brought a small amount of maize, but that was soon eaten. In desperation many were forced to drink their own urine. Many Dinka people fell down and did not get up. There were thousands of them on the long march either south or towards Ethiopia where they hoped for life. And they were starving.

Young boys banded together, marching along and clinging to their dreams. Makech, one of the Sudanese students, told me of their conversations as they kept close together walking along roads lined with the dead. They imagined fields of flowers and they were playing in them, playing at soccer.

They did not to know that many of them would spend the next twelve or fourteen years in a camp and maybe die there. They were fierce in their hopes. One of them carried a gun. They had heard of the enemy raiding the defenceless people and carrying away the women and boys their age as slaves. They fought the fear but along the road gossip travelled quickly and reignited their anxieties.

They closed their minds to the very worst things. All they thought about was food, and staying alive. They prayed to their God, often. They knew that land was the most precious thing of any country and they were being forced from it.

They knew the awful truth - the honoured person in their land was not honoured in a foreign land. They feared that they would become scavengers, seen as lazy and as useless as a piece of garbage but they said little to one another.

In their minds they were not becoming homeless. They were becoming displaced. In their villages they were happy and comfortable. They did not long for another life. They had order and discipline within tight traditional customs.

But all that they had known as normal and stable had been ripped from them in a deliberate attempt to de-humanise them. They were the Lost Boys.

At night the fleeing Dinka tribes lit fires to protect themselves from lions and other flesh-eating animals that had grown used to easy pickings. It was around the fire one night that one of the boys heard about the murders of his mother and father. An old woman from his village saw it happen. He cried bitter tears, but now he finally accepted his fate. He was an orphan who would no longer feel the love of his parents. He had two choices, to live or to die and he placed his life in the hands of God.

After months of travelling, the boys reached the camp of Kakuma.

During my talks with the students I discovered one of the Lost Boys of the Sudan and this is his story.

He was born in 1976, a Dinka child born from the village of Bor in Southern Sudan. He grew up in a family of five; three brothers and one sister. Life in his village was ordered and predictable and he had a happy childhood learning many of the traditional ways and playing with his friends.

At Christmas time the villagers killed many big beautiful bulls, maybe as many as a hundred. Then the people all came together to celebrate a gathering named barmat. They remembered the ancient god named Mangok. He was an angry and quick tempered god who would respond to anything they did wrong.

Someone had been selected from the clan to speak on behalf of the god. This was not witchcraft. He would speak in a soft and lovely way to represent the voice of the god. He used to speak to the boy's father and had been selected by many clans and sub clans.

The young boy knew that there was witchcraft in the village, but that it was a bad thing concerned with envy and jealousy. The witch, known as an apeth, could be a man or a woman and people were frightened when they saw the witch. If a woman gave birth to a beautiful baby or if someone had anything beautiful in their life, it was hidden from the apeth. These people were not common, maybe one of them lived in each sub clan. The boy learnt from an early age not to be a target for their eyes.

Since he had been a very small boy he had believed in this god. Christianity came to his village because a Dinka man was rumoured to have discovered a piece of wood floating on the river. It was covered with writing that told them about Christianity.

In 1987, when he was ten years old, his life changed forever. Friendly soldiers came to the villages to talk to the people convincing them of a plan to remove all the young boys from the surrounding villages and take them away to a place of safety where they would receive an education. The war was expanding and the boys needed to be protected. No one suspected that there might be another reason for this mass exodus.

All boys from the age of nine and above were collected together until there were thousands of them. The boy left his village in October. He didn't cry as he thought of it as a great adventure with an education at the end of it. His mother didn't want him to go as he was the eldest in the family and the chief male provider as his father had died several years before of a disease.

He patiently explained to his mother that if he remained he would be the only boy of his age in the village. He would be lonely and without male friends. His mother gave him a white bedsheet made of cotton with which to cover himself at night on the short journey to the school. He wore shorts, a shirt with long sleeves and no shoes. She prepared bread made with maize and oil and put it inside a plant gourd so that he could eat during the walk.

The boys gathered together to wait for the thousands of other boys from the many surrounding villages and then they left, singing loudly as they walked away. The long walk took six days and didn't end until they reached the desert of Ajager.

Remaining excited at the prospect of school, they grew hungry and thirsty, never anticipating such a long walk. Finally, hot and exhausted, the singing died away and thousands of weary boys lay down in the flat desert and waited for water. A tanker arrived, and replenished they walked on. But soon they again became desperate with thirst.

Many boys fell to the ground unconscious but others, including the boy I would later meet as a man, drank their own urine. Further down the road they discovered patches of mud and ate that. They still trusted the soldier, but they begged to return home.

The reply was always the same. "No, no. Just two more kilometres away. It won't be long now."

They encouraged the boys and carried guns so there was no argument. If any of the boys quarrelled amongst themselves the soldiers slashed at them with sticks and they soon began to realise that they were receiving discipline. They began to hear the words 'Minor Boys' and that name stuck with them.

Finally eighteen thousand boys trailed into Pibor, a town in Southern

Sudan where a tribe named Murle lived. These people were very hostile, but the soldiers protected the boys from them. They shot an antelope and it made him very sick. He fell unconscious and his elder cousin had to carry him until he recovered.

From that place they came to Pochalla and to the town of Anyak. Many of the boys were very upset, continually asking questions of the soldiers. From Pochella, on the border of Sudan and Ethiopia, they crossed a wide river to Panyido. Here he made friends with another boy who played games and swapped stories with him. His new friend had left his own village when he was only seven, his only possessions being a tin and a nylon bag. This incredible friendship was to survive eighteen years and be rekindled on another continent, but they weren't to know at the time.

Their route took them into Western Ethiopia. It was a green and tropical country that was very far from the boys' villages. This was where the first camp was made in terrible conditions. The numbers of boys increased as the second group of boys joined them. The United Nations High Commission for Refugees (UNHCR) provided basic food for the thousands of boys, but the hardships were unbearable.

Many times when the boy lay down to sleep he woke to discover a friend who had died or was dying of disease and starvation. As one friend from his village lay dying the boy tried to comfort him, listening patiently to the ramblings and pleadings for his parents, his homes and for love. This scene was to be repeated many times with many other friends.

When epidemics broke out, he was unable to dig graves as he was too weak and had no means with which to break open the hard earth. So he pulled the wasted bodies into the bush and they lay unburied.

The boys lost feelings and hope. Some went mad, shouting out in the night for their mothers and fathers. The boy did not cry because he knew that crying in his heart was greater than shedding tears. He recognised it as a deep sorrow that would perhaps never leave his heart. In the beginning he had cried when he saw his friends and relatives dead, but then as more and more people he had become attached to died he lost many of his human feelings and became numb. As time went on if they suffered from hunger many of the boys did not pray and sometimes they cursed God.

When the trucks arrived with grain the boys would pick up every individual grain, roasting them on the fire and eating them. They were always hungry. They were trained to lie and say they were simple parentless refugees, as the truth might have meant no more food. The truth was that when the UNHCR left the camp around three o'clock each afternoon the thousands of boys were taken to the bush and trained as boy soldiers. They carried guns made of wood and trained for three months.

There were bigger boys and smaller boys. Bigger boys were trained first and the boy felt angry as he wanted to join in. These older boys received full military training. Later it was his turn and some of the boys liked the training as it resembled a game. Boys from seven to eleven years of age trained in the rest time of the older boys. They stayed in the camp for four years, during which time many of the older ones were marched away to fight on the front line with the regular soldiers from the SPLA. Thousands of them died as they were too young and eventually they were removed from the front line. It was at this camp that he made a special friend, another lost boy.

In May 1991 the war broke out in Ethiopia and the long journey of the group that would become internationally known as The Lost Boys began as they retreated back to Sudan along with two hundred and fifty thousand other refugees. The boy ran overnight along with thousands of terrified and starving people to Gilo where they crossed the river. Many boys and women drowned here but the boy stayed with another group who returned to Gilo for food. He then ran with around twelve thousand boys from the seventeen thousand that had started out, back to Pochella, a village just inside the border of Sudan. There was not a single girl in the massive group.

They were taken from Pochella to Buma and then to Magoth where they were attacked by a hostile tribe called the Taposa. The boy escaped in the night, stumbling over the dead bodies of his companions, numb with fear and devoid of feelings of compassion. Too much had happened to him and his childhood was lost forever.

The diminished group finally reached the desert where the Red Cross discovered them. In 1992 they came to Narus on the border of Sudan and than Kenya where they spent three months. They built shelters but their stay did not last long. The Arabs took over so once again they were on the run back to the Kenyan Sudanese border. Their feet were bleeding, their starved bodies were covered in rags, their skin was covered in sores and some were naked, but they were frighteningly accepting of their fate. The boy had long ago ceased to believe in life. It was now only a matter of when and how he would die.

In May 1992 the UNHCR once again the discovered them. They were taken to Kakuma camp, where they set about building shelters from young trees.

Some of the boys started to play soccer and the boy joined in. Many of them quarrelled and remained unsettled. The boy watched two of his friends simply walk off into the desert and vastness of Sudan away from the comparative safety of the camp. Some of them left in the night to rejoin the army, for that was now the only life they understood.

But many of the boys stayed and waited. Thousands of the boys were accepted by the United States in a special humanitarian intake beginning in 2003. Some, like the boy who told his story to me, married in the camp and had children. Some waited and grew into men that regained their ability to love and feel compassion again, but will carry with them forever the unbelievable cruelty and violation of war. Some still wait.

It was in Kakuma that the two friends separated. The Lost Boy was sent to Community Group Eleven and his friend was placed in Community Group Four for minor boys. They had shared all their sadness and the separation was hard to bear.

Twelve years passed until they met again. The Lost Boy had left as a refugee to live in Adelaide, South Australia. He was studying English when one day the classroom door opened and in walked his friend of long ago. They immediately recognised each other and they hugged and jumped up and down with happiness.

'Where have you been?" each cried.

At the time of writing they still share the same classroom and I often see them sharing their experiences with each other. They are easy with each other and each time they meet they shake hands and pat each other on the back as if to reassure themselves that such a miracle has taken place.

They have hope for the future again, even as they never forget the ones they knew who weren't so lucky

The Tin

Eighteen years ago he left his village along with hundreds of boys, women and children. Arab soldiers attacked them. The village houses were burnt and many people were murdered.

He began the long walk to Ethiopia that would take him more than three months. He never saw his parents again. He was seven years of age and in his hands he carried his only two possessions, a nylon bag and a metal tin. He knew that on the journey he must lie on the nylon bag when he could rest so the scorpions could not sting him when they came above the ground. The metal tin would be used to scoop up water from muddy pools and rivers.

He trailed after the bigger boys, always hungry and always exhausted. It was September when the village ceased to exist and the long trail of people walked away from the lives they knew forever. The rainy season was approaching.

The walk was very difficult. As far ahead as he could see was a slow moving snake of Dinka people. Glancing behind him the people stretched into the distance and he never saw the end of the line. They would all experience the threat of wild animals including lions, hyenas and other carnivores. These animals grew fat on human flesh, easy pickings from the human trail.

The little boy tried to keep to the centre of the group of villagers he was walking with for he feared the parting of the tall grass on either side of the road. The roaring of the lions hidden from their view terrified everyone.

Ahead of him he heard the screaming of his people when a lion suddenly came out of the grass and jumped onto one person. In an instant he was dragged off. When the small boy saw this he screamed loudly along with many others. He saw the blood on the road as the line broke up and scattered in every direction, for the people had nothing to defend themselves with.

As they moved slowly along the road the people grew weary. The little boy was wide-awake with fear, staring into the grass to each side of the road for any sign of movement.

An old man slowed down near the end of the line, exhausted by the continual walking. For a short time he was on his own. A lion and lioness both emerged from the grasses and pounced on him, dragging him off.

Many of the Dinka people died from hunger and thirst, falling down as they walked. There was no way to lift or carry them because everyone was too weak. So the dead and dying were left at the side of the road and the little boy walked past them, staring at their twisted bodies and lifeless eyes, knowing their fate.

He was a helpless boy of seven. He couldn't do anything to help and he did not have the comfort of a mother or father. Sometimes he shared food with the group; grapes and fruit growing wild by the sides of the road and leaves and roots of trees.

Sometimes they were lucky as a small animal ran blindly into the mass of people as it tried to reach the other side of the road. With cries of delight the creature was quickly killed and eaten but these occasions were rare.

The boy grew hot and sick as he struggled to keep up with the others. At Pibot he knew that he could no longer walk, for his chest hurt and he was very feverish. Several women looked at him but turned away. He had pneumonia. There was nothing to eat but the hide of a cow and this was soaked in a small amount of precious water until it became tender. Then it was cut into strips and boiled for soup.

People sat on the dusty ground and silently sipped at the soup for they could no longer swallow even if there had been solid food. Their throats were swollen with dehydration, but they struggled to drink the liquid not knowing when they would next have any nourishment.

The boy was given a little of the liquid as he lay curled up on the ground and then he slept. He awoke to silence. The entire group of people had moved on and he was alone. Behind him he could hear the snap of bones as yet another lion feasted on a human body, but he was too sick and feverish to feel anything. Seven others remained behind, all too weak to continue. He slept.

As night arrived he woke to discover that he was entirely alone. The others had walked on. He looked around hoping to see at least one other person, but the place was deserted. Swarms of mosquitoes covered his thin body but he was too weak to swipe them away as they fed on him. He could hear the brittle snap of bones as a nearby lion continued to consume its victim.

Weak and helpless, he lay amongst the bushes and slept on his nylon bag. In his hand he clutched the tin. The morning came and he sat up to look around. The sounds of the bush had eased into a frightening silence as the sun began to rise. Struggling to his feet he began to walk slowly and painfully until sunset.

It was a question of life and death now. He wouldn't be afraid of anything ever again and he wished he could die. By night-time of the second day he approached the tall grass. He began to push through it. He saw the long necks of the giraffes and in the distance he heard elephants. He could see their tracks and droppings, broken branches and footprints. All around him he could hear the sound of animals. He could track the route of his people too, but they were too far ahead of him.

As night came the boy knew that he must find a safe place to sleep. The darkness came rapidly, but the boy spotted a large bush on the left side of the road. He crawled inside, pushing his way through its thorns and twisting branches.

Deep in the bush he paused for breath. Then he spread the nylon bag on the ground and sat on it, not making a sound. He now began to think about water. His body was very hot. He wondered what to do.

He took the tin and urinated into it. There was very little liquid and as he sipped it burnt his lips. It was very hot and bitter but he drank it anyway. Then he sat quite still for twenty minutes thinking about his village, his dead parents and his terrible situation before finally he lay down on the nylon bag.

All around him were the rustling sounds of the wild animals hunting and feeding on each other, but despite this he eventually fell asleep. In the morning he crawled out onto the road, but exhaustion and starvation made him very weak. As he struggled to stand upright his feet became entangled and he fell.

The tin rolled forward on the road, scattering the dust. The nylon bag fell behind him. He stared forward at the tin. There was no time to turn back for the bag. Every movement took away his energy. So he followed the tin and once more he clutched at it, this insignificant belonging from his village and his family.

He walked for three hours until a group of Dinka people finally caught up with him. They led him towards a river where many others were resting. When he saw the water he moved forward slowly and dipped the tin into the swamp and mud of the riverbank. He dipped the tin into the water three times but then he stopped. He may have only been seven, but he was wise enough to know that if he drank more he would die.

Many people joined them to wade into the water. He looked up at a tall fellow who stood in the swamp staring at him.

"Please boy, let me have that tin to drink water." And leaning towards the boy he took the tin from him.

The boy watched the tall fellow walking away carrying the tin. His tin from his village – and his last link with his home - was gone forever. He was sad. First his nylon bag and now his tin. He looked down at himself. His clothes were rags hanging from his skeletal body. Yet still no tears would come.

The people decided to cross the river at this point and others joined them until the banks were covered with thousands of people. The boy sat silently in the mud and watched this movement. He saw the natives who were not his people. They were the Anyuak people of Ethiopia and they carried boats with them. They used their tiny boats to cross the river and many drowned as boats capsized in the rushing waters. The boy remained empty handed and automatically became part of the crossing, swept along in the human tide.

But when they reached the other side, it was not a destination. The walking simply began once again as the people had heard of a camp named Panyido. This had been set up for refugees and the UNHCR was providing food. When they finally reached the camp there was actually very little food, but soon supplies came. Medicine and clothes were handed out. A school opened and the boy began to learn English. Here he stayed from 1988 until 1991, making friends with the other children.

In 1991 war broke out again. The people from the camp collected their few belongings and ran from the camp in the face of approaching soldiers. They followed a route named the Gilo Route, where they crossed the raging Gilo River. Hundreds of people drowned here and those who reached the other side, including the boy, ran every day during May and on until July in an effort to escape the soldiers. There were very savage lions on this route, hunting by day and hungry for easy pickings. The road was muddy and the grass on its verge was very tall and bright green – the perfect hiding place for the lions to stalk their prey.

Finally the people reached Pachalla in Sudan. The Arabs had chased them up the Gilo and many drowned as they tried to escape the bullets. As they ran they could no longer carry their babies with them. People became separated and as they grew weaker they threw their babies into the bush where lions fed on them.

Upon reaching Pachalla they were met by the Red Cross Society, who fed them. Tents were erected, as there was sufficient grass to cut with pangas. The people built shelters with the long grasses and crept inside for shelter and rest. Beans, maize, oil, mosquito nets and other useful things were handed out to the war ravaged people.

Several months later they reached the relative safety of Kakuma Refugee camp where he lost his friend The Lost Boy. By strange coincidence they found themselves meeting yet again at the College in Adelaide, although each had not known the whereabouts of the other.

At the time of writing this story they remain firm friends. The

Lost Boy is married and has two fine children, one of whom was born at the Kakuma refugee camp. The boy with the tin is single, but loves his new land and treasures his special friendship with another man who shares his suffering and loss of childhood.

Today they are seen together at the College and whenever they meet even if only a day goes by, they shake hands and smile. Both their journeys were long and terrible and no words are needed between them. Such incredible childhood lives no longer need to be spoken about to others, yet both of these young men are anxious that I tell their stories.

To see them in print means they will never be forgotten. And they hope that readers can gain strength from their experiences, for it is amazing and almost unbelievable that they survived and that they continue to have dreams and hopes for their future lives.

Slavery

It was daytime in his village when they came on horseback wearing uniforms and carrying guns. The Dinka villagers ran in every direction, unprotected and terrified as the Arabs were on a raiding party.

At the age of thirteen he knew war, famine and death, but his village had escaped violation until now. Everyone scattered. Shots were fired. The mothers were killed and the girls beaten and dragged off. He was running in every direction to avoid capture. He was tall and strong for his age, confident that he could escape capture, hoping to escape in the dust and chaos.

At the back of his mind he knew that he would either be taken for training on the front line or used as a slave. He had heard of these things from people who had been to the nearby city.

A horse pounded beside him and he looked up into the cold eyes of an Arab rider and knew it was all over. Escape was impossible. The rider dismounted, gathered the boy's thin body under one arm and threw him onto the horse.

This was how he lost his freedom and his family. He held onto the rider, crying all the time terrified lest he fall and be trampled under the horse's hoofs. One day's riding took them from the village of Magai to Wau. The man had selected him from the running mass because he was strong and tall. He would become the man's boy, looking after his cows and sometimes goats and sheep.

The man never spoke to him but took him to one of his wealthy houses where guards provided protection to all those within. He was the only slave in the household.

Days later, numb with fear of what might lie ahead for him, he met other boys out on the land looking after cattle. Together they talked about escaping.

One boy kept his distance, crouched on the ground, eyes down. Later they became friends as the silent boy began to trust him. They were from separate clans but the Dinka language was spoken with pride.

One day the boy asked him, "Have you ever been put into electricity?"

The boy was startled by this question, turning to the others for an explanation. They confirmed the awful truth of torture by electricity, for several had experienced this, but they refused to give him any details. The boy grew very scared, not understanding their meaning from their hazy explanations.

One night the Arab came for him, ordering him into a taxi. The driver took them into the town, driving through the labyrinth of streets, which the boy tried to remember. He dare not ask where he was going.

Leaving the driver waiting in the car, the man pushed the boy in front of him up many stairs in a large building. He could hear strange noises, but could make no sense of them. Finally he entered a long room that had been divided into cubicles.

The man ordered him to pick up the electric wires, which he was forced to wrap around his head, body and between his legs.

Even now he was puzzled and no one spoke. The man simply stared at him then walked away. He hobbled to the door and saw the man go to a large box on the wall. He pulled down the switches then walked away.

The pain was unbearable and the boy's screams were so loud that finally he could no longer hear himself.

Far away he heard other noises that did not sound human. They were more like the cry of animals in the bush. Slipping in and out of consciousness, it was the strange burning smell that finally awoke him. Through the sharp searing pain he caught the smell of burning flesh - his flesh.

He had no idea how long he had laid twisting and writhing on the floor. The man was standing over him, his cold eyes expressionless. He ordered the boy to remove the wires.

He could not recall how he crawled down the stairs to the waiting taxi. He crawled inside but the Arab did not come with them, walking off into the darkness.

Alone with the driver he shook uncontrollably. He asked the driver why the man had tried to kill him.

The driver spoke slowly and kindly. "My dear, you are lucky."

The boy asked him why.

The driver explained that the man had killed many people from the boy's tribe for his entertainment. "Maybe your God is too near to you."

He was not happy, but the boy grew brave, asking the driver what he had been thinking about when the boy was in the electricity.

The taxi driver drove for a while before answering. "I think it will be the end of you in the future, but by good luck you are still alive." He then asked the boy if he knew the city but the boy shook his head. He looked across at the taxi driver's kind face and knew that he cared.

At the house he was told to shower and then the driver brought some capsules and pressed them into the many wounds. There were many many burns and the boy was unable to move for three days and always in his mind was the knowledge that it would happen again and again until it killed him.

Finally he could hobble round and he was told to look after the cattle once again. He took the opportunity this presented and that was the day the boy escaped. He walked at night with eight other slaves to Akot, on to Bor, then to Juba and from there to Narus and finally on to Lokichokio.

The boys eventually came to the refugee camp of Kakuma. It had taken them five months of hunger, thirst and total exhaustion. They had survived on fruit from the trees, fish from the rivers and small dead animals they discovered on the long walk. They had crossed the White Nile by boat and here they had heard the sound of war and much crying. They avoided he area, always travelling south.

The boy remained in Kakuma camp before leaving for Adelaide, South Australia as a refugee, where he now lives happily, although like all refugees, never entirely free of his past.

Boy Soldier

He has been in exile for more than seventeen years. Even now he has never returned home. But in his own words, due to God's mercy and kindness he did not die. He did not want me to be surprised as he told me that there are things a man should pass through in this life. He asked me not to be shocked, but to learn from the telling of his story.

He explained that he put God as his helmet and shield for protection. And says that up until now God has helped him a lot, for the suffering of a child without a mother, father or close relatives was great.

He left his parents when he was eleven years old. This was because of the conditions that affected southern Sudan and the rest of the marginalised areas in the north like southern Arbour and the Nuba Mountains.

It was not his wish to desert his home. Nor did his parents reject him. It was because of the government of Sudan, who sent young and old men, women, boys and girls to the bush. They wanted Christians to become Muslim and would give them no chance to settle. It was very hard for Christians to settle as comfortably as Muslims and life in towns was miserable.

People were enslaved. Some worked hard and were underpaid. Some only received food if they completed a certain duty such as digging toilets and cleaning them. When the pit toilets became full someone had to remove the faeces by hand using a basket. They had to dig a new hole and empty the faeces into it. This was the life he was born into.

He explained his journey from home to Ethiopia. The Dinka people passed through Ajager, and through semi desert via Pachochalla and on to the town of Dimma. The journey was by foot and they travelled more than seven days in the desert.

In Dimma they were trained as soldiers for about nine months. Perhaps it made them fully trained as soldiers, but he had no way to compare or know whether nine months was enough to make him a good soldier. He then spent four years as a boy soldier in that area. It was not easy for him. He tried to learn from people who did not have the Dinka dialect. They were strangers to one another from different tribes and he was fortunate that he could speak Arabic, so he had another language with which to communicate.

In the camp the boys were well disciplined, respecting their leader and forming themselves into a platoon. If they fought or insulted each other they were punished and locked up for several days. They were alone without women in the camp because the situation and atmosphere would not allow this.

They used to cook for themselves by pounding maize with wood into grinding stones. This was hard for them as it is something they had never done before, grinding grain being women's work, but they adapted to it. Imagine someone who had absolutely no idea how to cook. They were forced to do what they did not want to do. Some of their people were old and could not cook, pound the maize, grind the grain or carry the water due to their ages. But the young boys were small so they cooked for the elders according to the Dinka norms and soon learned the necessary skills. They could not object because it was their duty, but it also made them feel proud because they were trusted to be responsible for their old people. But this did not last long as the older people eventually had to join in and do the duties as well. The memories of the old ways of caring for each other in a settled place were fading fast.

In Ethiopia they moved often because life was precarious and the natural resources of an area were quickly depleted, unlike life in their homeland. There were also frequent clashes began between Ali Mariam and the rebels called Orominya. This Tigrai revolution caused them to flee back to Sudan. The boy joined the battle. Perhaps it was because he was well trained; perhaps it was because he had no family nearby to advise him. He is no longer sure. But he remained, joining in the military exercises. His childhood and innocence had long vanished and there was nothing else for him to do.

No one could imagine the way they ran back to Kapoifa, South East of Southern Sudan, so close to the Kenyan and Sudanese border. The displaced people went up to Naruse, the displaced persons' camp and then they fled to Lokichoggio, in the border area between Sudan and Kenya.

The boy remained a full soldier participating in fighting with the National Islamic Front. He was overwhelmed by the excitement of holding a gun and doing the same job as the men did. He felt good and proud being a soldier. Things were not easy, but he endured the situation. He joined the division called Comescom for the first time, which in most cases dealt with heavy and big body weapons for air defence. For nine years he was locked into war, fighting and killing. He could not stay many days in one place, moving all the time and sleeping on the vehicle.

Eventually he was wounded on the forehead, which devastated his life and caused him great pain. He was dismayed because the fragment was very hard to remove from where it was embedded in the front of his skull. Even today part of it remains.

He got the wound on the 26th of February in 1997 in the desert of Pibor after the soldiers spent five hours walking to reach a town. They had walked during the night when they thought enemy were sleeping. The young soldiers had already planned to move further the following day. Then they would attack the town.

But in the night the enemy attacked the boys, wounding many people. This was the place where the shrapnel pierced his skull. They could not move further ahead, deciding to pull back and leave the town untouched. Unwisely, the soldiers followed the boys into the desert and one night they fell into the boys' hands. They were taught a lesson they would not forget. The boy soldiers killed many of them and he counted twenty-five bodies when he checked in the morning.

The group moved from place to place, always retreating. The enemy destroyed many things belonging to them, vehicles for example, using landmines. The boys could not be allowed to settle in and they were like the small chicken always being hunted by the huge eagle.

During all this fighting the boy tried to ask for help from his division commander so he could get treatment for his head wound, but it was quite difficult for him. The boy asked for money so that he could seek his own medication. As he could see that the boy was in terrible pain, the commanding officer told the boy that he could go, but with no money.

The by now demented boy did not insist on money for they were all in the same dilemma, out in the desert and with no funds of their own. Instead he swallowed his dismay and temper because there was no way that he could leave.

The pain in his head grew with the infection and eventually it was so great that he became really wild. All he could think of was to leave. People nicknamed him 'mad man' because of the way he behaved. They wanted to disarm him, but there was no way of doing it because he was so wild. What they finally did was to secure him by tying him to a stake while he slept, because they thought he would shoot everyone in his madness.

But such precautions were not necessary because it hadn't occurred to him to shoot them. Why should he? Who among them had harmed him? They were not wrong to command him to fight the Arabs. And it was the Arabs who had injured him. He had no intention of shooting his friends for it was wrong to do so before God. But his behaviour was so wild that they were not sure of what was in his mind.

He was finally released at the next town, where he traced an aunt who was working with the refugee program. She took him from the army and counselled him.

As a result of his aunt's intervention he gave up his gun at last and went to the camp of Kakuma, where he agreed to look after her children as she worked some distance away. He did this for three years, but it was very difficult. They were not his family or from his tribe and he was used to a life of such discipline that it was hard to live with the lively children, who he always saw as lacking the discipline that was the only way he knew.

Finally he had to accept the terrible lesson that he did not belong, as he was an in-law in the family and the children would not obey him as he expected them to. So much had happened to him, but this rejection of family and the realisation that he was an orphan was almost unbearable. A pain in his heart had replaced the pain in his head. He was alone in the world and even the running and fighting had stopped. His life seemed so empty now.

Fortunately an uncle then paid for him to attend a school in Uganda. Despite the fresh start, here he learnt all the difficulties that an orphan experiences without any family and accepted the way his life would be.

In 2005 he started his new life in Adelaide, South Australia and continues his education at a college that offers English for new arrivals. He mourns his family and he mourns the childhood he might have had, but not all the time because he chooses to fill his heart with hope for the future and determination to set and reach goals for himself. And for this he is truly inspiring.

The African Journeys

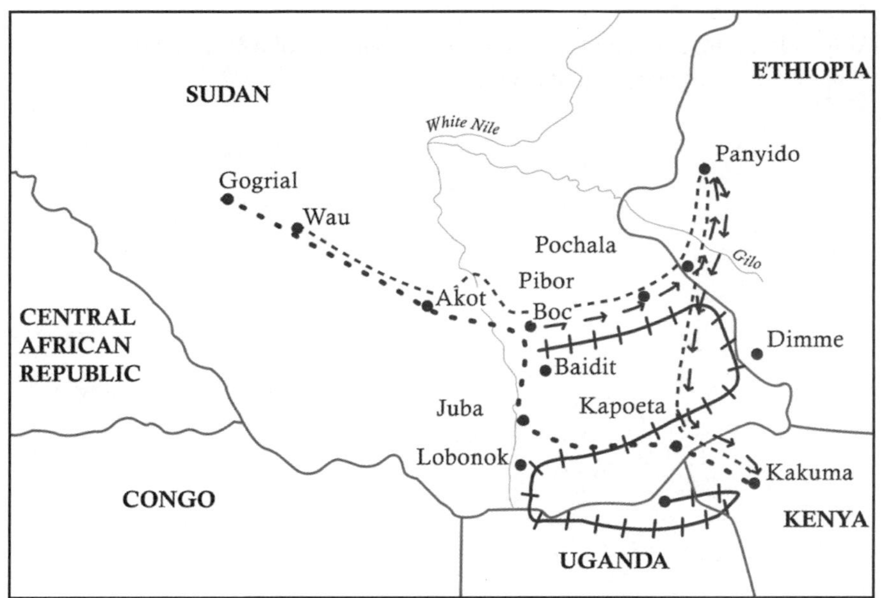

Carved into the stone directly above the entrance to the Senior College in Adelaide, South Australia are the words 'CARPE DIEM' (seize the day).

As I walk around in the recess and lunch times I see many Sudanese meeting each other, smiling and shaking hands. In Dinka they talk about their pasts and their futures. They embrace any new arrivals from the Sudan and every so often they see an old friend from Kakuma Refugee camp, which shelters thousands of displaced people. They are quick to tell me that they are not homeless but displaced because of war. They are a proud and beautiful people and I feel honoured to work with them.

They chose to tell me their stories in the hope that others will learn about their journeys and their dreams of a peaceful Sudan.

At long last I am beginning to find the great continent of Africa and the riches it has to offer through its many cultures.

Chapter Ten:

The Wanderer

The Wanderer

I met him in a language centre in South Australia, a man younger than me who could draw wonderful pictures on the blackboard in coloured chalks. I wandered across to his classroom one day after classes had finished and was startled to see a life-like tiger staring down at me. The artwork was quite incredible and I commented on it.

He laughed, picked up the board duster and swiped it away without a word. I learnt that day that 'no comment' was characteristic of this man. He smiled and laughed with the rest of us, charmed his students with excellent lessons, played his guitar and sang to them and invariably kept his classroom door closed on the establishment. I could relate to that in every way. It soon became apparent to me that his students loved him. A family had developed in his classroom and their loyalty was tangible.

He called me the 'Pommie' but in later years it became 'an honouree Aussie' which I took to be a compliment.

I watched him charge around, leaving quickly at the end of lessons unless there was a meeting. But he was always back very early every morning and preparing work in his classroom with the door shut. Meetings were another thing. He seemed attentive yet I sensed unease in him. He was there, but his restlessness had already timetabled him to be somewhere else.

I knew nothing about him but I sensed that in some inexplicable way we had things in common. What was it I wondered? Maybe it was this travelling thing, this promise to ourselves that what we owned ought to fit into a rucksack, a promise to seek freedom at all costs. Maybe the affection I felt for him was something to do with kindred spirits?

I never resolved this because out of the blue he began to talk about Cambodia. He wanted to go there. He began to learn Khmer and Vietnamese as he made plans, telling me that by the end of 1993 he would be gone. His goal was Cambodia, but he had been unable to secure work there.

I felt anger towards him for what I thought was an insane idea. How could he possibly go to Cambodia so soon after the terrible atrocities of the Pol Pot regime? Where was his sense of responsibility towards his family?

I had the pleasure of meeting his beautiful mother and handsome father at the graduation day at the end of the year. They walked across the yard to greet us, a handsome couple straight from a Somerset Maugham novel. It was obvious to me that they were still in love with each other. I watched to see their reaction towards their only child. With great pride father shook hands, firmly of course, with his son; and his mother, pretty as a picture, smiled gently, warming to the subject of her child.

I gently broached the subject of Cambodia but she smiled knowingly. "He'll do what he wants. We know that, his father and I. We hope he'll be safe. He'll stay in touch."

I thought of my own son and how I would feel if the day came when he wished to do something so adventurous. Would I be so generous in my thoughts?

I wondered about the start of his adventure, for it never occurred to me that this was a journey and he was not at the beginning of it. He told me very little about himself yet we remained good friends until he left the Language Centre.

From time to time over the years I spotted him in Adelaide on one of his return trips from either Cambodia or Vietnam. Occasionally he would ring me. Once he rang from the airport to say that he was leaving for Cambodia having spent a year on 40 US dollars a month in Nga Trang, Vietnam. I had little to say, I simply felt sick with anxiety. Later I heard about the death of his close friend in Cambodia and tried to contact him. In desperation I phoned his mother and heard the same gentle voice assuring me that he was fine. Only a few weeks before he had contacted them from Phnom Penh.

So I put him out of my mind until one day several years later I literally bumped into him in the Central Market in Adelaide. "How are you mate?" he smiled as he said his usual greeting.

I was ecstatic, hugging him while he stood patiently, letting me recover from the shock of seeing him alive but not so well. He had come back to Australia as he had a fungus growing in his gut, some tropical thing that had reduced him to skin and bone.

"Nothing to worry about," he laughed. "I'm going back soon."

We had a drink together and I invited him out to the high school where I was working. Sure enough he turned up for an entire day and freely gave his time to the many English as a Second Language students. He brought amazing photographs with him, at least thirty enlarged pictures that showed the psychological aftermath of the Pol Pot regime. Many students had seen the film The Killing Fields and thought they had some understanding, but these pictures further showed the terrible face of war. I remember several that showed paintings outside a cinema, but the subjects were drawn from the tortured minds of the people who had lived through such times. He slid the worst ones to the pack of the pile and did not show them to the students, several of who were Cambodians.

Then he was gone again and I never saw or heard from him until 2005 when he turned up teaching in a classroom near to mine at a senior college in Adelaide!

Little had changed about him. His beard had gone but he was still fit and lively. I spotted the guitar in his classroom and he complained that the whiteboards did not lend themselves to chalk drawings.

We shared the same office and we swapped our stories at every available moment. Fourteen years had passed and I was finally to discover all the answers that I had sought so long ago. And I was in for a big shock!

Within two days he had shown me the scar across his skull and neck, telling me quite blithely about the worms that had entered his brain and almost killed him. Later he told me in detail about this nightmarish experience.

I asked about his parents. His father had died very suddenly in late 2004 and that his mother was dying in a nursing home, one and a half years since his return from a year in Japan. For many months he visited her every weekend, but she no longer recognised him.

I asked if I could visit her and he seemed to like that idea. Unfortunately I never saw her again as within months she died and he disappeared from the college for several days.

She died the day before Mothers' Day and on the Friday morning he rushed into the College holding a single pink rose. He pinned it up on a piece of paper at the top of the stairs for all to see with his distinctive handwriting above it.

'Happy Mothers' Day to all our mothers.'

Then he dressed up in an apron and produced ice creams for both of our classes who were about to watch a very moving film called The Weeping Camel. He wanted to create the idea of a cinema and even brought a torch to shine on the students in the darkened room as he gave out the ice creams!

Then he called me into the office next door. "Just tell them I've had to go. Don't tell them where. I don't want them getting upset. They've had enough sadness in their lives. My mother is dying."

I didn't see him again for several days but when he returned, he was so sad and in mourning for his mother that only the students brought a smile to his face. Sometimes we would sit silently in the weak winter sunshine during recess and lunch breaks but we spoke very little to one another. Slowly we resumed our conversations and now he was prepared to tell me about his wanderings to many places long before I ever knew him. It was as if he was free to do so.

His ancestors came to South Australia in the second migrant ship, the Africaine, that sailed in to Holdfast Bay. His great great grandfather was a farmer at Two Wells before the family moved north. His father rode a Shetland pony to school travelling the six miles from Halbury to Balaklava. He came from stern country stock and was very proud of his country connections. His mother came from the Riverland and was one of ten children. Every Christmas their only child would work on one of his six uncles' fruit blocks at Renmark. He attended a school at Eden Hills near to his family home.

Many of his classmates were from The Stolen Generation who lived at Colebrook Home. Over the years hundreds of these children occupied this place. They had been taken from their families around Quorn and beyond and they were real bush kids. His first girl friend was Aboriginal and he loved his Aboriginal friends who sought the freedom of the outdoors, hating the trapped feeling of being shut up in a classroom. He desired that freedom too and also shared a love of drawing and music with them. His drawings consisted of cartoons whereas theirs portrayed nature. He admired their incredible eye for detail and related to them.

His parents had moved to Eden Hills after his dad returned from the signing of the peace treaty in Tokyo Harbour where his ship picked up Australian prisoners of war. He returned to Australia with tuberculosis and sought the fresh clean air of the hills. His parents were poor at this stage in their lives and used orange boxes for furniture.

He learnt independence from a very early age from 1957 onwards. That Christmas, at the age of nine, he was put on the train by himself to Renmark. It was one hundred and sixty miles and involved changing onto a bus half way through the journey at Morgan. He remembered crying the first time, but it was the foundation for a lifetime of independence and travel. He was of course an only child and had no sibling to confide in so he accepted this annual trip that went on for ten apricot seasons. Later, his first teaching appointment would be at Waikerie where his great grandfather was buried so there was a strong family connection for him in the Riverland.

The sense of travel and freedom, which stemmed from his mother's side of the family, gave him the mental freedom needed for a global traveller.

By the time he was fifteen he was playing top-level tennis and the urge to achieve and stay fit always prevented him from going down the dark road of depression or substance abuse in his future life. Fitness always drew him back to a life of normality.

His first classroom was covered by travel posters that he scrutinised, determined to visit some of the places he saw. Three years later he was off on his first overseas travels aboard a ship with a school friend, resigning from the education department in order to realise his dreams.

His parents were a tremendous back up for him, always encouraging him to follow his dreams. A year in Southern Africa changed him in many ways; his hair and beard grew long and he was hardly recognisable. He spent some time riding a motorbike that gave him the freedom he wanted, but within a few months he had abandoned that form of transport, hitchhiking up through Botswana and Rhodesia. He was almost shipwrecked on the Skeleton coast of Namibia as a result of accepting a passage on an 1898 schooner. She logged five hundred miles into the sea journey, but the wind changed and the engine broke down, leaving the schooner becalmed for five days. In potential danger as they drifted helplessly into the shipping lanes, he faced the strong possibility of a disastrous collision during the foggy nights. Fortunately his mate cranked up the diesel engine all but a hundred metres from some pretty serious rocks and they chugged back to the small fishing village of Swakopmund on the coast of Namibia.

His serious travelling had now begun.

Hitchhiking back across the desert, he finally reached Cape Town, where he put his sporting experience to good use by looking after the diving and tennis departments of a sports store. He immediately became the superior of his black colleague and friend Abrahim Benjamin who had a white father and black mother. He preferred to be called a 'non black', which he explained as 'Cape Coloured'. Chinese people were called 'black'. Japanese people were 'white' and apartheid was insanely active.

At this time Nelson Mandela was in jail on Robben Island, which he could see from his home, and there seemed to be no crack in the system to allow real identity for black people.

The young Aussie was fed up by the entire system as he had grown up with Aboriginal children and played footy with Aboriginal boys in the Riverland in South Australia. After a year of apartheid he left for the Canary Islands, hoping to pick up a passage on a yacht heading for the Caribbean. He wound up in the United Kingdom.

Once again on the move he headed for and worked in Nottingham,

Manchester and then Newport in Shropshire with his friend Smiley from Australia and another mate, a Pommie whom he'd met in Durban in South Africa. Smiley was straight out from military service in Vietnam, a real loveable larrikin. So began five years of adventures. They bought an old Ford, which they called Fred Prefect and took it onto the M6 where it promptly ran out of water. Laughing, they peed into the radiator, which enabled them to reach the next service station!

He worked in a hotel in Keswick in the Lakes District.

During the next few months he and the Pommie lad travelled to Munich for the Olympics, sleeping in a huge circus tent with hundreds of others. They were fed with the left over food from the Olympic games and had many adventures. A close school friend from Adelaide joined him and together they travelled across Europe for several months until their money ran out. They ended up in Denmark, sleeping in a plastic tent!

Finally he left his friend and returned to Cornwall in England. He grimly remembered lying in a little tent eating banana sandwiches on his own as the rain poured down inside and out! It was time for work once again. He never sent for money from his parents as this was his adventure and if it meant doing without so be it.

He made for Aviemore in Scotland, a climbing and ski resort, and lived there for three winters, falling in love with a beautiful highland lassie. But he still wandered, though always returning, as he loved her. Once he arrived at Aviemore from Ireland in the middle of the night. He put a ladder up against her window and delighted her by suddenly reappearing!

But the desire to be mentally and physically freed grew strong again, calling him to the United States with two of his mates. He was always happy to hit the road, but this time he was risking a special thing in leaving his love behind.

When they finally reached America they travelled through the United States to Mexico, back up to California then on to Vancouver, where he drove trucks in a copper mine on Vancouver Island.

Eventually he returned to Aviemore to the girl he loved and together they travelled to Jersey where they both worked. Yet again he shot through, using an old post office van as transport. Freedom always beckoned. Finally the brakes failed on the van and he limped back using the gears and handbrakes until he reached Jersey.

Returning to Scotland where they became engaged, he planned his return journey to Australia while her family imagined a romantic sea journey on a great ocean liner. But he had a wish to travel overland to Australia and they did just that, having incredible adventures in Turkey, Iran, Afghanistan, India, Nepal, Thailand and Malaysia.

Reaching Perth they were totally broke, a result of blowing the last of his cash on a stereo system in Singapore! It took them three days to hitch hike from Perth to Adelaide.

They arrived back on his mother's birthday, Remembrance Day, November 11th, 1975. She worked as a waitress in a city restaurant and he scored a job driving a tractor, cutting the vast lawns of Flinders University as he couldn't get back into teaching. They moved to a flat near the university and eventually he landed a job at Scotch College, where the principal knew of his sports history.

He lost the lovely girl through his unpredictable behaviour and was devastated, but she refused to ever come back to him. His parents loved her too, but she eventually moved away to New South Wales.

For the next five years he had another girl friend. They travelled together until he landed a job in Nauru. Before reaching Nauru, they had headed off to Thailand where they split up. He travelled alone through Burma, down the east coast of India to Madras then boarded the Ramaswaram ferry where it was every man for himself. On he went to Colombo where he picked up his mail and found a letter from his ex girlfriend. She was living with an American in Kandy and she took him in, leaving with him to travel up the west coast of India.

They split again in Bombay as he had always vowed to follow the Nile from its source, but recognised that it could be too rough a trip for her. She accepted this and they made plans to meet up again in England.

Flying on to the United Arab Emirates and then Saudi Arabia, he tried to disembark at Jeddah but did not have a visa. He ended up in Khartoum and a Sudanese guy he'd met on the plane invited him to stay. After a night's rest he journeyed out to the desert to take up an invitation to visit a Bedouin sheik and his three sons who had studied in Germany, England and Paris. They dealt in selling and training camels, putting on camel races for their Australian visitor, taking him into the desert in a Land Rover to the mausoleum of the sheik's father. Then they travelled a further ten kilometres to enable their six riders to race their camels back to the monument that stuck out like a point in the desert and acted as a finishing line.

A week or so later he returned to Khartoum where he slept on the floor of the university for a night, resting in readiness for the long journey to the source of the Nile. Early next morning he boarded the windowless train to Wadi Halfa, a massive journey of fifty-two hours.

They experienced incredible dust storms and he wished that there was glass in the windows of the train. He slept on the sand with the locals when they made stops, taking with him a few sandwiches. The next morning he fulfilled a dream by following the Nile from its source.

He caught a ferry - six hundred Sudanese and one white man and went past the ruins of Abu Simbel, a magnificent sight thousands of years old. These ruins had been moved from the Aswan Valley when the Aswan dam had been filled with water.

The Sudanese sat on the roof singing beautiful songs, but the women were hidden away, always. Sleeping with the singing still ringing in his ears he felt strangely contented and fulfilled by this amazing experience. Alongside hundreds of Sudanese men he felt safe and slept soundly.

At Aswan who should come out of a hot little cabin but a British soldier in civvies, wearing a pith helmet from colonial times. He had a long cigarette holder, was very posh and squinted at the only other white man, put his head back and roared with laughter! They both went straight to a coffee shop and smoked a hookah together, exchanging their experiences and plans for the future. Of course they became good friends, ending up travelling together. They explored the Valley of the Kings and all the time the Aussie was amazed that there had been two of them aboard that ferry and neither knew of the other!

They parted in Cairo - him to England and the Aussie to Israel, moving overland through the Gaza Strip to Jerusalem. He travelled on through Rhodes and Athens, hitching through Yugoslavia and Austria to Vienna, Amsterdam and finally to London and on to Aviemore where he met up once again with the girlfriend he had split with in Bombay.

They flew back to Adelaide, but within a week he was teaching in Nauru, an island in the Pacific famed for its bird shit. His fourteen-month certificate of employment could not be broken, but his mate was so desperate to leave that he deliberately smashed his hand against a wall, breaking two fingers!

Nauru was a mecca for ex patriot gossip and the Aussie and his Aussie mate provided some more! There were over fifty single beautiful airhostesses living on the island and very few relationships survived.

Nauru had become incredibly rich at that time. If a deposit of bird shit, (guano) was found on anyone's tribal land the owners gained instant wealth. It was a place of extremes, poverty and obesity lived side by side with incredible wealth and the island was littered with blue Fosters' beer cans!

The Aussie loved his work, escaping each weekend to dive in the beautifully warm seas. He dived on Japanese war wrecks in the Solomon Islands during a holiday break. During his classroom work he tried to restore the legends of Nauru to barefoot Nauruan children, lost through the influence of Western excesses.

He was unaware that Cambodia was growing closer to his future and his destiny was back in Adelaide as in 1983 there was a huge influx of Cambodians from Kao-i-Dang, a camp in Thailand.

Upon his return from Nauru, an intuitively wise staffing officer named Anne Sexton lined him up for work at the Thebarton Literacy Centre, where he once again met up with his mate from Nauru. He made his first contact with new arrivals from Cambodia.

When his Cambodian students had sufficient English to tell him about their experiences they stood up one by one in no order and advanced towards him, literally pinning him against the blackboard in their haste to tell what had happened to them. They were the most horrific tales imaginable.

The next five years were spent in language centres meeting Vietnamese boat people, Chileans escaping Pinochet, El Salvadorians, Armenians and many cultural groups from the former Yugoslavia.

His days were filled with the madness of war. Yet Cambodia itself eluded him. It was not yet time.

Austin, Texas was his next appointment in 1989, where he took up a teaching position at Texas Junior High School. It was at this school where he experienced the most extreme racism since South Africa.

During black history month, which was held across the USA, he gained permission to show Alex Hailey's Roots. This was a worry for the principal, as the black students knew next to nothing of their ancestry. They had no more than a passing knowledge of the fifteen million black Africans who were kidnapped from the West Coast of Africa to be used as slaves in America, and certainly knew no details or individual stories.

The TV series, the guitar and his fantastic blackboard murals completed a month of incredible realisation for his students. Accused by some Hispanic students of being racist, he tried unsuccessfully to explain his intentions to both them and their parents in an awkward confrontation.

BLACK HISTORY MONTH

During this difficult teaching time in Texas, news broke out on a playground massacre of a number of Cambodian kindergarten students. He read with interest of the thirty thousand Cambodians who had settled in the San Joaquin Valley in California and knew that his experience could be useful in the situation. Determined to teach there, he flew to Los Angeles, hired a car and drove up the west coast to Stockton in California where he had six interviews in a day! He soon heard that he had won a position.

Over the long summer vacation he visited the Galapagos Islands in the early days of tourism, then travelled across Ecuador and to a village on the Amazon, ending his trip through Lima, Cuzco and Machu Pichu and onto La Paz in Bolivia.

Ahead of him lay the fascination of Cambodia, and his new position would reinforce his passion for that country because while working with the gentle students in California he became friends with a Bilingual School Service Officer, who he would later come across in Cambodia, and they talked in detail about the country where he wished to live.

My understanding of his complex journey had now reached full circle. He was prepared through his travelling, his tolerance and love of all cultures, the deprivation and hardships during years of wandering to live in a country weighed down by the horrors of war. The students' stories, his parents and friends' love added to his mental strength, which he needed to make that first journey in 1994. Sharpened and stripped clean of westernised frippery, his senses heightened, his survival skills developed to a high level and stripped clean of personal relationships, he needed no anchor. His wandering had led him inward towards a country that would touch his soul.

Finally he reached Cambodia in 1994 and would return many times, living there for four separate years. When I first came across him in the Language Centre he was already making plans to leave Australia, earnestly learning Vietnamese. Everything that had happened to him in the travelling he had experienced had led to this moment when the plane touched down in a country ravaged by war.

In 1994, thirty of the world's most wanted criminals lived there. He met up with his close friend Big John, whom he had met the previous year in Vietnam, encouraging him to come to Cambodia. They would share the year of 1995 together under its spell, becoming brothers to each other. John was also a veteran traveller and knew how to survive in the most difficult circumstances. Once they had settled into rooms in the capital of Phnom Penh they sat out at the pavement stalls drinking beer and observing a totally different and very fragmented culture.

It was out on the roadside of the city that they heard a strange story told by an ex pat. Had they heard the tale of the Australian who had visited a leper colony, asking for a doctor to cut out a large skin cancer from his leg? Evidently he had even drawn a line with a felt tipped pen around the area and urged the apprehensive doctor to 'dig deeper' to make sure he had removed all the cancer.

"That crazy man was me", interrupted my friend, explaining to the men that he had lived with skin cancers for years. He's had at least a hundred and fifty stitches in his face and neck over the years, but doesn't feel sorry for himself, explaining that his experience of this taught him two things. The first was to do something immediately about the skin cancer and secondly to value every precious second of every day.

Then the three men drank their beers and had a good laugh about it.

All around them they could see the evil of paedophiles; old men coming out of hotels with little boys of eight or nine, dull eyed and expressionless. In return for their services they received a small amount of money for themselves or their families and food.

There were thousands of prostitutes choosing this life as an alternative to hard labour in a rice field, or because they had been sold by desperate parents or bought and sold and bought again by traffickers. AIDS was rife. Death amongst expatriates was a regular occurrence, resulting from AIDS, alcohol and sometimes by the odd stray bullet in crossfire that occurred night and day. Often someone in the bar would say, "Another one has bit the dust."

They lived amongst gunfire night and day for six months and occasionally a grenade rattled the windows of their rooms.

The Aussie lived with the extremes of life and death night and day until it became his world, a terrible and evocative drug that enveloped him completely.

All this time he strove to teach and help his students. An AK 47 gun-fight started outside a beer garden one night, continuing for two to three hours. He and John picked up their drinks and casually went inside knowing that what went up must come down! It was also a common practice for men to fire into the sky, at times doing it to frighten away evil spirits. It was the lawlessness of the Wild West and once night came to the city, the locals drew their concertina steel doors shut.

The people lived in fear but the ex pats felt that they were invincible - it was still only fourteen years after the Pol Pot Regime was at its peak and the Khmer Rouge were very active.

On the roads leading out of the city the United Nations soldiers were on their hands and knees scraping inch by inch for mines. They would clear a fifty-metre stretch and at nighttime the road would be re-mined.

Amputees hopped about everywhere, open sewers flooded with the rains and dead rats were washed onto the roads and pavements. Destitute people slept in the streets and many died in the cold period of December. The city flooded with tropical downpours half a metre to a metre deep. People had to wait for it to subside before they could continue on their journey.

One major survival skill was to use black humour about the bizarre incidents such as the man who fried on the overhead wires and stayed there for two days flapping about like a piece of brown paper. It was not uncommon to see bodies after armed robberies.

Still my Aussie friend continued to teach and care for his students. One day the students all hit the floor at the sound of gunfire and he was so ignorant of the dangers within his classroom where he thought they were safe that he continued writing on the blackboard.

It was a bizarre existence for most of the time he was cut off from the events of the outside world. Cambodia was his world. Most expats had cable TV however, so they were well informed. The Phnom Penh Post was full of local events, which took precedence over global affairs.

At one stage he taught the Members of the National Assembly and the Senate. The daughter-in-law of the King was also in his class, arriving in a car with darkened windows and always with a bodyguard. One day the car arrived without her and instead the armed guard came in with a box of spring rolls specially prepared for him at the palace. He was asked to teach these VIPs because he was a non-political animal and very tactful in his approach. While he filled his hours teaching, his friend Big John read books for most of the day and voluntarily built a playground for mine victims who had lost limbs as he had worked as a builder in London and Germany.

Most weekends they would explore the seedier side of the city, easily imagining it being emptied during the years of the Pol Pot Regime. For three years, eight months and twenty days it had remained totally empty - the city of ghosts. The buildings became mouldy, churches were demolished, and trees were chopped down. But strangely the beautiful coconut trees around the city survived.

The remnants of this hellish time were still evident when the two men lived there. Dust from the unsealed roads was everywhere, in the computers, in his lungs, coating his clothes for the city was landlocked.

The Aussie never once thought about material possessions or Australia apart from infrequent calls or messages to his parents. He maintained constant empathy with the people, who were gentle and ripped by war and he lived as one of them, ate their food, was drawn into their culture. He regularly mixed socially with his students. He was slowly and inevitably being drawn into another world.

Despite the appalling human devastation he found beauty there. The sunsets were incredible, the town was often flooded by a golden glow illuminating the Buddhist temples and the palace. The Tonle Sap River flowed through the centre of the city changing directions in November when floodwater rushed into it.

He thought so many times how beautiful the people were, so gentle yet so capable of violence. He thought about the future success of his students for at that time between eighty and ninety percent of Cambodia was comprised of illiterate farmers. His commitment lay with his students and they knew this. He began the IELTS (International English Language Testing System set by Cambridge University), working initially from one book. His students were orally sound, but their written work was poor and they had poor knowledge of geography and world events. By introducing the IELTS, he gave them a framework for their study and an internationally recognised goal for them to strive for.

In 1995 things began to change, though subtly. There was still gunfire, but it grew less and less. Vans with heavily armed soldiers still cruised the streets, but change was coming to Cambodia. He recalled the devotion of the Khmer people to their ancestors; it was vital to their wellbeing. He listened carefully to the funeral music in the streets recalling its incredible sadness. Khmer people he had befriended died of malaria and tuberculosis. And he mourned them.

At the end of 1995 he grudgingly left the country he loved so much to return to Adelaide. This was in order to secure his permanency in teaching in South Australia. But Australia was now foreign to him. It was this year when I met him in the Central market in Adelaide looking skeletal but very anxious to return. Tragically, and suspiciously, his close friend Big John died in Phnom Penh while he was in Adelaide. It was during a particularly violent political change.

In 1998 the Aussie returned again to Cambodia to teach, carrying with him the sad memories of a man who had been his brother. One day he went to the edge of the Killing Fields, which were knitted with the bones of the dead and saw the Toul Sleng School used as a centre for torture by the Khmer Rouge but he had no wish to ever return.

He had met a former student who introduced him to her family, recalling a beautiful man with massive dirty hands who prepared a meal for them. The first course was frog soup with cooked frogs floating in the liquid. He had eaten frog many times before but in times to come he would often wonder if this was the source of an illness that was to have a huge impact on him.

Months after the frog soup meal he awoke one day with double vision. He wondered if he had had a stroke. He was working extremely hard preparing students for the IELTS examination and had two months to go before the final exam. In that particular class were three of Cambodia's eleven psychiatrists who were dealing with eleven million psychiatric problems. There were also several doctors, all selected by AusAid from the Cambodian ministries. One student tried to study with the knowledge that his brother had been kidnapped. The strain on the students was enormous so the Aussie said nothing about his eyesight.

But it got far worse. He saw two motorbikes, two TVs and he was annoyed because he had to squint to see normally. In the evenings he would sit on his balcony trying to puzzle out what was wrong with him. On his extreme vision to the right would be a man walking along. Twenty metres behind him would be another man. When the first man reached his mid range of vision the second man caught up with him and they became one. He didn't panic but he knew something was very wrong.

He saw a doctor who announced that he was working too hard and thought he might also have a detached retina. The ophthalmologist had been his former student; he'd graduated at Perth University and returned to Cambodia to help his people. He did every test possible but he confirmed that it wasn't a detached retina.

Finally he was referred to Sumitivej hospital in Bangkok, which took him away from his students. By this time his vision had deteriorated but he calmed himself while waiting in the deluxe room at the hospital. Fortunately he had private medical insurance that he had never used before.

As a result of an examination he was sent to the other side of the city for magnetic resonance imaging, at that time in the only machine of its kind in Thailand. After a few hours in the tunnel of the machine and injected with coloured dye, he was told to return immediately to the hospital. He was told that he could suffer a seizure at any minute as white spots had shown up on the MRI results. For five weeks he endured numerous tests to see if the spots were brain tumours or worms. He had a spinal tap, an internal camera investigation and a course of steroids, twenty-three a day, in case it was worms.

Lying back in his hospital bed, feeling disorientated and confused, he finally accepted the possibility of death. He was told that if it were tumours he would be lucky to have five years of life. He was already in touch with a top neurosurgeon in Adelaide as the neurosurgeon in Bangkok had discovered what looked like a tapeworm, visible to the naked eye and sitting near to the optic nerve and they discussed the possibility of it blocking the spinal column. He was warned that if the white spots were in fact worms they were feeding on his brain. When the steroids hit the worms he would certainly know about it. So his imagination took over, the situation growing into a nightmare.

During this entire nightmare he was on his own. He convinced the doctor that Halloween was very special in his culture and could he leave the hospital for a short time? They told him he could have just one beer, as the steroids would make quite a cocktail. Believing that he may have limited time did not panic him. He decided that he had had an incredible life so that night he hit the bars and had numerous beers before returning to his fate.

Drifting in and out of reality, he felt waves in his skull and on many occasions he felt as if his brain was moving! The top Adelaide neurosurgeons advised him by phone that they were very unfamiliar with such a case and to go ahead with the operation in Bangkok.

Every test right up until the time of the operation showed negative to worms and it began to look more and more likely that it was brain tumours. He accepted his fate. He received phone calls from far away, from his parents and friends and was far more concerned for their anxiety. He remembered little now as he drifted in and out of reality as the worms were hit by the steroids.

For some strange reason he wrote a letter to the Greater Mt Zion Baptist Church in Austin, Texas, and thanked them for accepting him when he went in to listen to their amazing gospel singing. He told them it was the most moving musical experience that he had ever experienced.

He wandered about his room waiting for the operation and the sky lit up with an electrical storm. A huge bolt of lightning struck outside the hotel and he smiled grimly to himself. He was searching for something, a private inner search as to his meaning on this earth. His biggest concern was for his aging parents.

He thought about the richness of his life and his birth date stamped on a marble that went into a barrel in 1968. All Australian males aged twenty whose number came up had won the lottery - one year of training and then Vietnam. He didn't win this particular lottery and had an indefinite deferral and no adventure. It had all been a roll of a marble.

As they wheeled him down the corridor towards the operating theatre his mate from Vietnam arrived and held his hand. He could hear the sound of saws working on other people in other operating theatres.

Then he went under. As he became deeply unconscious he saw a brilliant light. It was square and he was racing towards it. Suddenly it went blacker and blacker as if a sliding door was shutting out the light. He gained consciousness in intensive care and the first thing he said was "Is it a worm?" for if the answer was in the affirmative he would have a future.

The nurse held a viscous thing up in a bottle. "Here it is."

Back in the room the terrible pains started in his head. Slowly his vision returned. Many tests were done on the 'worm' that turned out to be a colloid cyst that had been with him since birth. All of the white patches were in fact worms, which were feeding on his brain and bringing him very close to epilepsy and total blindness.

Weak but hopeful for his life he finally left the hospital and was booked into a hotel. One the first night he ventured out to see the world he thought he had lost forever. He was too weak to stay out long, but on the second night he tried again. He had to return to his room after a short while.

Reception phoned to say that he had a visitor. A girl from one of the bars came up to his room and gave him a lovely bunch of flowers! He was very moved by this single act of kindness for she was simply a poor girl who worked in one of the bars and had overheard his story.

Head shaved and very thin, he had one burning ambition, to see his students before their final exam. He flew back to Phnom Penh and arrived there the day before the exam. His students had been very worried for they loved and cared for him. He didn't want them to suffer for they had been through so much to reach this point in their lives - broken down air conditioners, kidnapping, violence during the 1997 political change and the massive effort to prepare for study in Australia was enough to cope with without the worry of what had happened to him.

But he was a wonderful teacher, the man I first saw all that time ago drawing a tiger on his blackboard back in Adelaide, and he returned to give them that last little bit of confidence before the all important day.

And then he came home to his parents, who had given him the confidence and the freedom to begin his life of wandering. To give them comfort in exchange for the gift and inspiration they had given him. And even then his students came first…

I am proud and honoured to work with him and if I try to tell him so he simply smiles at me and says his usual dismissive word, which denies any open praise, "Whatever!"

BLACKBOARD TIGER

Courage

No one owns your time
you have no finishing line
and at the roll of a dice
you pick up a bag and go.

to new destinations, infatuations,
passions for unknown places,
midnight impulses where shapes
turn to faces and you jump
your ghost ship

You took the train to the bush
for ten apricot seasons
killed the fear of solitude
lost a child's self pity
learned the worth of every
second of every day.

What drove you to Cambodia?
A thrill of dancing in gunfire
to test your invincibility?
Shuffle the pictures
save the bitter ones for later
the women who parade bandoliers
of shells like jewels
Men so gentle yet busy with death
and sullied with funeral music to
care
about lost temples and mouldering
shrines,

Courage is a fine guardian
during a boy's journey
in manhood, no safety against bullet
a smile no insurance in the blood
of sunset executions.
when Buddha became an amputee,
a pile of fractured skulls.

Courage is reckless when you ignore
gunfire
and continue to teach amidst the
mayhem,
incomparable when you queued with
children
in the killing fields to speak with
ancestors
and taught them of legends wiped
from schoolbooks.

Ryan Ó Conaill

'My bridge crosses and empty line
My mind wanders a lonely track
I have painted companions on my path
Intoxicated conversations with wine
And over my shoulder thrown my finger ring
And discovered a taste for wandering.'

About the Author

JANICE MADDEN was born in Crewe, England.

She has worked for many years as a teacher specialising in English Literature, Creative writing and English as a Second language. Her stories are usually autobiographical, revealing her skilled observations, her generosity of spirit and empathy for human kind.

By Janice Madden:

Circles Within Circles
Knights of the Road

For more information please visit www.janicemadden.com